# Design

Admiral John Fisher in his first tour as First Sea Lord had been the driving force behind the design and construction of HMS *Dreadnought*, the world's first all-big-gun battleship to be completed. As soon as the design for *Dreadnought* was selected for construction, the so-called 'Battleship Committee' launched into the task of selecting a new armoured cruiser design. In the previous seven years the Royal Navy had built seven classes of armoured cruisers. Just as British pre-dreadnought battleships had a mixed battery, so too did the RN armoured cruiser designs. Although the 'County' class and 'Improved County' class had mounted all-6in guns for the 'Counties' and a combination of 7.5in and 6in guns for the 'Improved Counties' as an economy measure, the other five classes had the tried and true 9.2in gun as their main guns with 6in or 7.5in guns as the secondary. The Imperial German Navy had followed suit but their designs used 8.2in guns for the main battery and 5.9in guns for the secondary.

## BLÜCHER

If the *Dreadnought* marked a watershed in battleship design, the new armoured cruiser selected by the committee was an even greater change from previous armoured cruiser designs in that it incorporated all big guns in the design but of 12in battleship calibre – far larger than the 9.2in guns of previous designs. The chief constructor, Phillip Watts, was in favour of a uniform armament of 9.2in guns for the new design, making them an armoured cruiser equivalent to the *Dreadnought* concept but Jackie Fisher insisted on the 12in gun as main armament. By weight of his personality and position as First Sea Lord, he got his way and the *Invincible* class was created. At first they were still called armoured cruisers but the novelty of having a uniform 12in gun armament on ships faster and larger than previous cruiser designs actually created a new type of warship, which became known as the battlecruiser. Although details for the new *Dreadnought* design were published, Fisher chose to employ misinformation in regard to the *Invincible* design. It was deliberately leaked that the new armoured cruiser design would have 9.2in guns, rather than 12in guns. The German navy swallowed the bait and accordingly designed a new armoured cruiser with uniform cruiser armament of 8.2in guns. This became SMS *Blücher*. When the German navy finally tumbled to the truth, it was too late. They were committed to a design that was not only significantly slower than the *Invincible* but also far weaker in armament.

Although often described as a hybrid and neither fish nor fowl, the *Blücher* still serves as the link between armoured cruisers and battlecruisers, a stage jumped by Jackie Fisher for the Royal Navy. SMS *Blücher* was authorised in the 1906–1907 program. In appearance and turret layout, the ship was a miniature version of the *Nassau* class battleships. Built at the Kiel Navy Yard, the cruiser was laid down on 21 February 1907, launched on 11 April 1908 and completed on 24 March 1910. In an odd ammunition supply arrangement, the two forward beam turrets had to receive their ammunition from the magazines

**Below:** Although *Blücher* had an all-big-gun armament, the guns were 8.2in – obvious here from the small size of the turrets – compared to the 12in of the first British battlecruisers. This made *Blücher* a design anomaly, but she nevertheless spent her war years alongside the battlecruisers of I AG (*Aufklärungsgruppe*, known in English sources as 1st Scouting Group), after service as a gunnery trials ship before 1914. The main features of the ship are clear in this pre-war view of the ship, entering harbour with the crew manning the side. *(Bundesarchiv 134-B0041)*

## DIMENSIONS AND DISPLACEMENT

| Class | Length oa | Beam | Draught | Load | Deep Load |
|---|---|---|---|---|---|
| *Blücher* | 530.5ft | 80.3ft | 26.3ft | 15,590 tons | 17,250 tons |
| *Von der Tann* | 563.3ft | 87.3ft | 26.6ft | 19,100 tons | 21,802 tons |
| *Moltke* | 610.3ft | 96.8ft | 27ft | 22,616 tons | 24,999 tons |
| *Seydlitz* | 658.2ft | 93.5ft | 30.5ft | 24,610 tons | 28,550 tons |
| *Derfflinger* | 690ft | 95.2ft | 27.3ft | 26,181 tons | 30,223 tons |
| *Hindenburg* | 698.2ft | 95.2ft | 27.3ft | 26,513 tons | 31,000 tons |
| *Mackensen* | 734.9ft | 99.7ft | 30.5ft | 30,510 tons | 34,742 tons |
| *Ersatz Yorck* | 748.1ft | 99.7ft | 30.5ft | 32,972 tons | 37,402 tons |

located under the two aft beam turrets. Each round was placed on an ammunition rail, which provided a conveyor belt type of arrangement. This placed ammunition in transit outside of the armoured barbettes and turrets protected only by the thinner side belt armour. This design error was directly involved in the loss of the ship at the Battle of Dogger Bank. *Blücher* went through a lengthy trials period, starting on 1 October 1909 and later participated in gunnery trials. However, the *Blücher* did have one characteristic which was superior to the British battlecruiser designs: her armour scheme. The significantly larger and more powerful *Invincible* and following *Indefatigable* classes both had 6in armour belts, which was the same as the last armoured cruiser design. With *Blücher* the German designers incorporated a main armoured belt and turret armour of 7in (180mm). The wisdom of the heavier armour was amply demonstrated in 1915.

## VON DER TANN

With the first true battlecruiser design, officially described as a *Grosse Kreuzer*, German designers turned the table on the British. One could see the size of a ship and count her guns but could not see or measure armour protection. British writers did not know that the *Blücher* had a stronger armour scheme than the British battlecruisers and assumed a 6in belt as in previous armoured cruiser designs. 'Of the successors of the *Blücher*, being German *Indomitables* or Dreadnought-cruisers, little is known. The *Von der Tann*, launched in March, 1909, is to be completed in the spring of 1910,' commented *The Naval Annual 1910*. This first mention of *Von der Tann* credited her with twelve 11in guns, presumably arranged as the 11in guns of *Nassau* or the 8.2in guns of *Blücher*. Nothing was mentioned about armour, except in a table at the back of the volume, which listed an 8in belt for *Von der Tann*, but put in the caveat 'particulars doubtful'. With the *Von der Tann* German designers set the pattern for the entire line of battlecruiser construction for the High Seas Fleet. The ship had minimal superstructure, presenting a low target, inferior main armament to British contemporary construction (11in versus 12in) but most importantly, far superior protection. Although always classified as battlecruisers, the German designs were more akin to fast battleships. Gone was the mistake of the wing turrets of *Blücher*; instead the *Von der Tann* improved upon the British practice of spacing amidships turrets far enough apart to allow cross-deck fire. The *Von der Tann* was a direct reply to the *Invincible* class but was far superior in every category but main armament.

On 25 March 1908 *Von der Tann* was laid down at the Blohm & Voss yard in Hamburg, five days after the completion of HMS *Invin-*

**Below:** As the first true battlecruiser in the Imperial German Navy, *Von der Tann* attracted a lot of attention when she visited Spithead for the Coronation Fleet Review in June 1911. This quarter view is one of many photographs taken at the time and shows clearly the appearance of the ship in her early years. The large louvered ventilators were a prominent feature of this and subsequent German battlecruisers. Two of the 8.8cm SK anti-torpedo-boat guns can be seen in casemates on the quarter. *(©National Maritime Museum N04918)*

**Left:** A bow view of *Von der Tann* at the Coronation Fleet Review at Spithead in June 1911. Note that the ship is not yet fitted with anti-torpedo nets and booms. The forward pair of 8.8cm casemates are fitted in a vertical section cut out of the flare of the forecastle, but later ships simply mounted them behind hinged panels flush with the hull. Like all major ships of the Imperial German Navy, *Von der Tann* carried a heraldic device either side of the stemhead – usually the family coat of arms of the person the ship was named after. *(©National Maritime Museum N11083)*

*cible*. She was launched a year later on 20 March 1909 and completed in September 1910. Not only did she greatly improve on the characteristics of *Invincible* but also incorporated novel design features – she was the first German capital ship to use turbines instead of triple-expansion reciprocating machinery, and four propeller shafts. During construction, in an effort to counter rolling characteristics encountered in the *Nassau* class battleships, Frahm anti-rolling tanks were worked into the design. However, certain design sacrifices were made to achieve the end result. Since German ships were intended to operate in the North Sea instead of the worldwide arena, they could be given a lower freeboard and poorer crew habitability than the corresponding British equivalent. *Von der Tann* did have a raised forecastle deck, but she was still wet compared to British battlecruisers with their higher freeboard. Another sacrifice was in the hull frames. In order to save weight, lighter hull framing was worked into the ship, compared to British designs. The consequence was that upon firing her main guns, the ship shook considerably.

## THE *MOLTKE* CLASS

To make up for the time lost in the design and construction of the *Blücher*, even though *Von der Tann* was still on the building ways, the design of an improved *Von der Tann* was being completed. Less than eight months after the start of *Von der Tann*, the first of this class was laid down on 7 December 1908, also at the Blohm & Voss yard. This was to be SMS *Moltke*. Similar in appearance to the *Von der Tann*, the *Moltke* class was larger and heavier: displacement jumped from 19,400 tons in *Von der Tann* to 22,616 tons in *Moltke*. Much of the displacement increase resulted from a hull size that went from 562ft 9in length and 87ft beam in *Von der Tann* to 610ft length and 96ft 9in in beam. With an increase of almost ten feet in beam, the *Moltke* could be given an even greater number of compartments, further increasing survivability of the design. Although turret and barbette armour stayed on par with 9in, the *Moltke* class increased the thickness of the main belt from 9.84in in *Von der Tann* to 10.75in. One need only compare the armour belt of *Moltke* with the contemporary British battleship HMS *Neptune*, laid down six weeks after *Moltke* with an 11in armour belt, to see that the German battlecruisers were fast battleships. In contrast to *Moltke*, the second class of British battlecruisers, the *Indefatigable* class, simply carried over the same 6in armour belt from the *Invincible* class, with *Indefatigable* being laid down on 23 February 1909, two and a half

**Below:** *Moltke*, the second battlecruiser design, introduced a fifth turret, superfiring aft, which was an innovation in the German navy. The forecastle deck was also carried as far aft as the quarterdeck, allowing the secondary casemates to be fitted one deck higher, which made them more effective in a seaway. The ship is seen here steaming out of Kiel before the war, showing the prominent black extension fitted to the fore funnel in 1912 and the additional platform for the admiral's bridge.

**Right:** The forecastle of *Moltke* as built, without the funnel cap and extended bridgework. Compared with their British opponents, German battlecruisers had very little superstructure, which gave them the advantage of a lower silhouette but at the expense of good sightlines for their commanders. *(Bundesarchiv 134-C0526)*

months after *Moltke*. The increased size of *Moltke* not only allowed greater armour and survivability to be worked into the design, but also permitted greater offensive capability. The 11in gun was retained but in a new longer L/50 calibre of slightly improved performance, while the increased hull length allowed a fifth turret to be added, located in a superfiring position aft. This made *Moltke* the first German warship with superfiring guns. Although *Moltke* was laid down before the first British ship with superfiring main armament, HMS *Neptune*, both powers were late in adopting this subsequently standard practice, as the United States Navy had used superfiring turrets from the start of the *Dreadnought* era. One other improvement in offensive abilities was the placement of the secondary 5.9in casemate guns. The deck break from forecastle to main deck in *Von der Tann* came at the forward superstructure but the forecastle in *Moltke* was extended to the after superstructure before the drop to the quarterdeck. As a consequence the secondary guns of *Moltke* were located one deck higher than those of the preceding design.

The sister ship to *Moltke* was SMS *Goeben* and since she was in the 1909 construction program instead of the 1908 program with the *Moltke*, *Goeben* was laid down exactly one year after *Moltke*, on 7 December 1909, also at Blohm & Voss.

## SEYDLITZ

Only *Goeben* was included in the 1909 program as the rest of the capital ships were battleships. The 1910 program saw a new design developed from the *Moltke*. Laid down on 4 February 1911, the *Seydlitz* was a one-off design, which sought to address weaknesses of the previous class. To

**Below:** *Moltke*'s sister *Goeben* was to experience a very different war from all the other German battlecruisers. She is seen here during one of the many visits made to Mediterranean ports between November 1912 and the outbreak of war, when she evaded pursuit by the British and was turned over to the Turkish navy. She not only survived the war but also outlasted every other battlecruiser ever built, not being broken up until 1971. *(©National Maritime Museum L5846)*

**Left:** As completed *Goeben* was almost identical to *Moltke*, but the fore funnel extension was shorter and the after funnel had no cap, unlike the flat but protruding device fitted to her sister. Note the forward 8.8cm guns exposed by the open flaps; at speed and/or in a seaway, the ship's bow wave rendered these mountings useless, and they were removed during the war.

**Left:** *Seydlitz* at speed, possibly during trials. The main structural difference with her predecessors was the addition of a forecastle deck running as far aft as the bridge – earlier German battlecruisers were very 'wet' ships, and the increased freeboard forward was an attempt to ameliorate this condition.

provide a drier forecastle, it was raised one level, giving the *Seydlitz* two deck breaks, one at the end of the forward superstructure and the second at 'D' turret, compared to the single deck breaks for the *Von der Tann* and *Moltke* classes. Length again increased to 656ft but in an odd retrogression for German designs, beam was reduced by three feet to 93ft 6in. This was done to provide a better underwater hull form for higher speed. During trials *Seydlitz* attained 28.1kts, developing 90,000shp. In partial compensation for the narrower beam, the armour belt was increased to 11in maximum thickness and the maximum armour on turrets and barbettes to 10in. *Seydlitz* retained the same main turret arrangement as the *Moltke* class but the gun was mounted in an improved turret. Completed on 22 May 1913, *Seydlitz* was the last battlecruiser to join the High Seas Fleet before the Great War and was flagship of the scouting squadron when the war began.

**Above:** A very clear broadside view of *Seydlitz* hove-to in the fjord-like bay of Kiel. The crew is manning the side, probably on the occasion of Kiel Week in July 1913.

## THE *DERFFLINGER* CLASS

Although *Seydlitz* was a superb ship, it was clear to the German Admiralty that their battlecruiser designs were falling intolerably behind British battlecruisers in terms of offensive abilities. HMS *Lion*, laid down in November 1909, upped the stakes by increasing the main armament of British battlecruisers from 12in to 13.5in guns with a far greater shell weight, improved accuracy and longer range. It was one thing to accept a trade-off of 11in main guns versus 12in guns in British battlecruisers, given the advantages achieved in German protective systems, but any greater inferiority was not acceptable. A total redesign of the battlecruiser type would be required, resulting in a complete break from the initial *Von der Tann/Moltke/Seydlitz* series.

Every major element was reconsidered for the new battlecruiser. The first priority was the main armament, the 12in (305mm) L/50 gun used on German battleships being the final choice. To save weight the echeloned wing turret arrangement of the previous designs was eliminated and four centreline turrets with superfiring 'B' and

## BUILDING DATES AND FATES

| Name | Builder | Laid Down | Launched | Completed* | Fate |
|---|---|---|---|---|---|
| *Blücher* | Imperial Dockyard, Kiel | 21.2.1907 | 11.4.1907 | 24.3.1910 | Sunk 24.6.1915 |
| *Von der Tann* | Blohm & Voss, Hamburg | 28.3.1908 | 20.3.1909 | 1.9.1910 | Scuttled 21.6.1919 |
| *Moltke* | Blohm & Voss, Hamburg | 7.12.1908 | 7.4.1910 | 30.9.1911 | Scuttled 21.6.1919 |
| *Goeben* | Blohm & Voss, Hamburg | 7.12.1909 | 28.3.1911 | 2.7.1912 | Scrapped 1971 |
| *Seydlitz* | Blohm & Voss, Hamburg | 4.2.1911 | 30.3.1912 | 22.5.1913 | Scuttled 21.6.1919 |
| *Derfflinger* | Blohm & Voss, Hamburg | 1.1.1912 | 12.7.1913 | 1.9.1914 | Scuttled 21.6.1919 |
| *Lützow* | Schichau, Danzig | 15.5.1912 | 29.11.1913 | 8.8.1915 | Sunk 1.6.1916 |
| *Hindenburg* | Imperial Dockyard, Wilhemshaven | 30.6.1913 | 1.8.1915 | 10.5.1917 | Scuttled 21.6.1919 |
| *Mackensen* | Blohm & Voss, Hamburg | 30.1.1915 | 21.4.1917 | N/A | Broken up 1923-1924 |
| *Graf Spee* | Schichau, Danzig | 30.11.1915 | 15.9.1917 | N/A | Broken up 1921-1923 |
| *Ersatz Freya* | Blohm & Voss, Hamburg | 1.5.1915 | 13.3.1920 | N/A | Broken up 1920-1922 |
| *Ersatz Friedrich Carl* | Imperial Dockyard, Wilhemshaven | 3.11.1915 | N/A | N/A | Broken up on slip 1919-1922 |

* Commissioning dates

'X' ('C' in German terminology) turrets incorporated. With the inclusion of two heavier superfiring turrets in the new design, something had to be done to cut topweight, so the raised forecastle was eliminated, making it the only flush-decked German capital ship design to see service in the First World War. The name ship of the class was SMS *Derfflinger*, laid down on 1 January 1912, followed by SMS *Lützow* in July. Length was increased by over 30ft compared with *Seydlitz*, with *Derfflinger* measuring 690ft. Beam was increased to 95ft but the design was still narrower than the *Moltke* and *Goeben*. The armour thicknesses were also increased, with maximum belt thickness of 11.8in and turret and barbette armour of 11in. Machinery was designed to use oil, as well as coal, although Germany had no internal source for fuel oil. The Frahm anti-rolling tanks fitted in *Derfflinger* were omitted in *Lützow*, allowing the ship to mount one extra 5.9in gun on each broadside for a total of fourteen.

Another unit of this class was laid down on 30 June 1913 as SMS *Hindenburg*, but the design was slightly modified for this third ship, just as HMS *Queen Mary* varied from the *Lion* and *Princess Royal*. The *Hindenburg* was 9ft longer and accordingly heavier than her two sisters. *Hindenburg* also developed 9000shp more power and therefore was one knot faster than *Derfflinger* or *Lützow*, but she carried the same fourteen 5.9in guns as the latter.

## THE *MACKENSEN* CLASS

SMS *Mackensen* and her three sisters, *Graf Spee*, *Prinz Eitel Friedrich* ('Ersatz Freya') and *Fürst Bismarck* ('Ersatz A') represent the last class of German Battlecruiser actually launched during the First World War. A fifth ship, 'Ersatz Yorck', was ordered for the class but subsequently redesigned to accommodate 15in guns and would have had a different appearance. Although described as battlecruisers, the *Mackensens* were in reality the ultra fast battleships of their day. *Mackensen* was designed with a 12in armour belt with up to 13in of armour on her turrets. True contemporary battlecruisers – the *Lion* class and HMS *Tiger* (9in belt, 9in on turrets, IJN *Kongo* (8in belt, 9in on turrets), HMS *Renown* and *Repulse* (6in belt, 11in on turrets) – would have been completely outclassed by *Mackensen*'s protection. She is more appropriately compared to contemporary battleship designs: USS *Texas* (12in belt, 14in on turrets), HMS *Queen Elizabeth* and HMS *Revenge* (13in belt, 13in on turrets), IJN *Fuso* and IJN *Ise* (12in belt, 12in on turrets), USS *Nevada* (13in belt, 16in on turrets), and USS *Pennsylvania* and USS *New Mexico* (14in belt, 18in on turrets). Only the later classes of US battleships had superior protection to that of

**Below:** The *Derfflinger* class marked a radical break with previous battlecruiser designs in the adoption of a flush-decked hull, with an innovative longitudinal system of framing that offered significant weight-saving. This quarter view shows the name-ship at the beginning of the war.

**Right:** Like her predecessors, *Derfflinger* was a 'wet' ship at speed. During her first operation, the Scarborough Raid in December 1914, the ship encountered Force 7-8 winds and Sea State 6 waves, shipping a lot of water over the deck, but her captain reported that well battened-down the ship remained dry internally.

**Above:** *Lützow* differed from her sister in the additional admiral's bridge deck and yardarms X-shaped in plan view. As seen here at Danzig in August 1915, both funnels were jacketed for only half their height (as in *Derfflinger*), but as finally fitted out at Kiel the jacketing was extended to the top of the fore funnel.

**Left:** *Lützow*'s fore funnel was soon jacketed for its full height. She carried out trials at a far deeper draught than designed – as shown here – and in shallow water. The best recorded was 26.43kts, from which it was calculated that the ship might make 29kts in deep water.

*Mackensen*. The *Queen Elizabeth* class were the first true fast battleships of the dreadnought era, capable of 25 knots, but the *Mackensens*, with almost the same protection, were designed for 28 knots. With eight 13.8in guns, the class would have been formidable opponents for the Royal Navy.

All four in the class were laid down in 1915. *Mackensen* was launched on 21 April 1917 and *Graf Spee* on 15 September 1917. The other two were never launched, and work soon stopped on the first two in order to provide labour and material for German U-boat construction. They were never finished. *Mackensen* was listed as part of the fleet to surrender to the Grand Fleet in November 1918 but as *The Naval Annual 1919* stated: 'The battlecruiser *Mackensen* was not so far completed as to be ready to join the melancholy company of her impotent companions in internment.' The battleship *Baden* was substituted in her place. After the war consideration was given to converting the first three ships of the class into diesel-powered tankers (10 knots) of 18,500 tons but the plans were abandoned for lack of funds. All four were scrapped between 1920 and 1924. The profile for the *Mackensen* would have been very similar to that of the *Derfflinger* class but with a larger forward funnel. The *Mackensen* had one last impact on naval history: the design of

## ARMAMENT CHARACTERISTICS

| Ordnance | Class | Shell Weight | Range | Rate of Fire |
|---|---|---|---|---|
| 11in L/45 (28cm) | *Von der Tann* | 302kg | 18,900m | 1.5rpm |
| 11in L/50 (28cm) | *Moltke, Seydlitz* | 302kg | 18,100m | 1.5rpm |
| 12in L/50 (30.5cm) | *Derfflinger* | 405kg | 16,200m | 1.0rpm |
| 13.8in L/45 (35cm) | *Mackensen* | 600kg | | 2.5rpm |
| 15in L/45 (38cm) | *Ersatz Yorck* | 750kg | 20,400m | 2.5rpm |
| 8.2in L/45 (21cm) | *Blücher* | | | |
| 5.9in L/45 (15cm) | all | 46kg | 13,500m | 7rpm |
| 3.45in SK L/45 (8.8cm) | all except *Hindenburg* | 10kg | 10,700m | 25rpm |
| 3.45in Flak L/45 (8.8cm) | all | 9.5kg | – | 10rpm |

## MACHINERY AND PERFORMANCE

| Class | Engines | Boilers | Range | Coal Capacity | Shaft Horsepower | Max Speed |
|---|---|---|---|---|---|---|
| *Blücher* | 4-cyl VTE | 18 Schulz Thornycroft | 3520nm @ 18kts | 2260 tons | 34,000 | 24.25kts |
| *Von der Tann* | Parsons Turbines | 18 Schulz Thornycroft | 4400nm @ 14kts | 2760 tons | 43,600 | 24.75kts |
| *Moltke* | Parsons Turbines | 24 Schulz Thornycroft | 4120nm @ 14kts | 3050 tons | 52,000 | 25.5kts |
| *Seydlitz* | Parsons Turbines | 27 Schulz Thornycroft | 4700nm @ 14kts | 3540 tons | 63,000 | 26.5kts |
| *Derfflinger* | Parsons Turbines | 18 Schulz Thornycroft | 5600nm @ 14kts | 3640 tons | 63,000 | 26.5kts |
| *Hindenburg* | Parsons Turbines | 18 Schulz Thornycroft | 6800nm @ 14kts | 3640 tons | 72,000 | 27.5kts |
| *Mackensen* | Parsons Turbines | 32 Schulz Thornycroft | 8000nm @ 14kts | 3940 tons | 90,000 | 28.0kts |
| *Ersatz Yorck* | Parsons Turbines | 32 Schulz Thornycroft | 8000nm @ 14kts | 3940 tons | 90,000 | 28.0kts |

**Right:** *Hindenburg*, seen here running trials without the 8.8cm Flak mountings, was a modified *Derfflinger*, some 2.5m longer and incorporating a tripod mast with its massive control top; *Derfflinger* was fitted with a similar structure after Jutland. The ship never carried net defence equipment but was fitted to handle two floatplanes, stowed one either side of the aft funnel.

**Below:** After a short and largely uneventful career, *Hindenburg* is seen here entering Scapa Flow in November 1918 to suffer the indignity of internment.

## ARMOUR SCHEMES

| Class | Belt | Turrets | Barbettes | Conning Tower | Transverse Bulkheads | Decks |
|---|---|---|---|---|---|---|
| *Blücher* | 7in | 7in | 7in | 10in | 6in | |
| *Von der Tann* | 9.5in | 9in | 9in | 9.5in | 7in | 2.5in |
| *Moltke* | 11in | 10in | 10in | 10in | 8in | 2.5in |
| *Seydlitz* | 11in | 10in | 10in | 10in | 8.7in | 2.5in |
| *Derfflinger* | 12in | 11in | 10.2in | 11in | 10in | 2.5in |
| *Mackensen* | 12in | 12.8in | 11.5in | 14in | 10in | |
| *Ersatz Yorck* | 12in | 12in | 12in | 14in | 10in | |

the inter-war battleships *Scharnhorst* and *Gneisenau* was strongly influenced by the *Mackensen* design.

## THE 'ERSATZ YORCK' CLASS

There was one final battlecruiser design developed for the Imperial German Navy. Originally to be additional units of the *Mackensen* class, three unnamed ships were redesigned in January 1917 to carry eight 15in guns, as mounted in the *Bayern* class battleships. They were officially listed as 'Ersatz Yorck', 'Ersatz Gneisenau' and 'Ersatz Scharnhorst' (in theory, each of these was a replacement – 'Ersatz' in German – for a previous ship, hence the nomenclature). 'Ersatz Yorck' had actually been laid down at the Vulcan Yard in Hamburg in July 1916 but construction had been stopped after 1000 tons had been worked. The profile would have been similar to that of *Mackensen*, except there would have been a single, massive trunked funnel, instead of the previous two-funnelled arrangements. After the stoppage of what little work had been done for 'Ersatz Yorck', no other effort was expended on this class, as Germany just did not have the resources to complete the *Mackensens*, much less work on the new design.

# Careers

*Blücher* went through a lengthy trials period, starting on 1 October 1909 before commissioning on 24 March 1910 and later participated in gunnery experiments. When *Von der Tann* was commissioned, she and *Blücher* were assigned to the 1st Cruiser Squadron, which comprised the main units of the Scouting Force under Admiral Hipper, which provided the advance guard and reconnaissance for the battleships of the High Seas Fleet. As further German battlecruisers were completed, they too were added to the Scouting Force. The one significant exception to this pattern was the SMS *Goeben*, whose 60-year career, as the longest-lived battlecruiser, will be covered at the end of this chapter.

## COASTAL RAIDS

The German battlecruisers had not seen any significant action in the first months of the war. They were unable to respond in time at the Battle of Heligoland Bight, in which the British battlecruisers under Admiral Beatty had sunk several light cruisers and destroyers. They had put to sea in conjunction with sorties of the High Seas Fleet but there had been no run-ins with the Royal Navy on these occasions. Although Kaiser Wilhelm had ordered the German Fleet to act defensively with the battleships, in late October plans were laid to use the battlecruisers, plus *Blücher*, offensively in raids on the English coast. This was to serve as bait to draw out the British forces and hopefully reduce its numbers with submarines and mines or draw an isolated component into the guns of the German surface fleet.

Late in the afternoon of 2 November 1914, Hipper with *Seydlitz*, *Moltke*, *Von der Tann*, *Blücher*, light cruisers and destroyers had left the Jade for a high speed run across the North Sea during the night for a dawn raid on the fishing port of Yarmouth. The guardship, the aged cruiser *Halcyon*, was lucky to escape into the mist and the only opposition was provided by a few old destroyers and submarines. Hipper saw that he was just wasting ammunition on his tiny foes and turned back to Germany. As he left a few haphazard shells were fired off towards Yarmouth but all they did was to churn up some sand on the beach. The only loss was the RN submarine *D 5*, which struck a mine and sank leaving only four survivors. Three trawlers were also destroyed.

The Admiralty had been caught flat-footed, but Hipper was bitterly disappointed and embarrassed by the meagre results of the raid on Yarmouth. Plans were prepared for another raid in December with the targets a number of ports further north, closer to the base of the British battlecruisers, to try to provoke a response from Royal Navy heavy units. As the German force neared the coast they divided, with *Von der Tann*, *Derfflinger* and light cruisers moving south to Scarborough and *Seydlitz*, *Moltke* and *Blücher* heading for Hartlepool. A half-hour bombardment of Scarborough left 17 civilians dead and 99 wounded, and there were further casualties an hour later at Whitby.

Sixty miles north of Scarborough was the town of Hartlepool, which unlike Scarborough and Whitby, actually had legitimate military targets in the form of six docks, various foundries and mills, as well as a defensive force of two small cruisers, four destroyers and a submarine. It also had a shore battery of three old 6in guns, and in the event these were to provide the only effective opposition to the bombardment that began at 08:10. As *Seydlitz* and *Moltke* steamed slowly across the mouth of the harbour, *Blücher* glided to a stop to improve her gunnery. Two guns fired at the battlecruisers and a single gun at *Blücher*. The gunners managed to score some hits but did no serious damage, and at 08:52 Hipper ceased firing after 1150 shells had savaged the port. In all 86 civilians were killed and another 425 wounded. *Blücher* had been hit with four 6in shells while stationary, damaging one turret and knocking two 5.9in guns out of action, while killing or wounding nine of her crew.

By 09:30 the two German forces had reunited and headed back towards

**Below:** The Yarmouth Raid, 3 November 1914: seen from *Von der Tann*, the *Seydlitz* leads *Moltke* and *Blücher*. *Von der Tann* is cleared for action but the leads of the net defence gear clutter up the deck edge over the 5.9in casemate battery. *(©National Maritime Museum L5847)*

**Right:** The battlecruiser force en route to the bombardment of Scarborough and Hartlepool, 16 December 1914. Seen from *Von der Tann*, the line is led by *Seydlitz* with *Moltke* and *Derfflinger* astern.

Helgoland. Two days earlier code-breaking had warned the British that something was afoot, and Jellicoe planned to sortie the entire Grand Fleet but this was vetoed by the Admiralty. He was only allowed to use the Battlecruiser Squadron and one division of battleships, which took station on the Dogger Bank to ambush the German battlecruisers on their way back to Germany. The tactical command was with Vice Admiral George Warrender of the 2nd Battle Squadron, with Beatty commanding the battlecruisers, now reduced to four ships – *Lion*, *Queen Mary*, *Tiger* and *New Zealand* – as some of Beatty's ships had been dispatched to hunt Graf von Spee's force and others were still in the Mediterranean. As dawn broke on the 16th, the ten British ships approached Dogger Bank in ignorance of the fact that the High Seas Fleet, in distant support of the operation, was heading straight for them and only a few hours away. At 05:15 the screening forces of both sides made contact, but the German fleet commander von Ingenohl convinced himself that this was the screen for the entire Grand Fleet and ordered his fleet to retire, thus losing the greatest opportunity that the High Seas Fleet would ever have to decisively engage an isolated portion of the Grand Fleet.

Now the tables were turned and Hipper was isolated, with ten capital ships between his force and safety. As Hipper steamed towards home at 23kts, his screen of light cruisers encountered Beatty's screen, also of light cruisers, in poor visibility. However, communication errors led to the recall of the British light cruisers to the battlecruisers, which allowed Hipper to evade Beatty and then in turn Warrender's battleships, and they safely made it back home.

Outraged British newspapers branded the German raiders as baby killers, but there was as much disappointment about the RN's failure to bring Hipper's ships to justice, although they would be even better prepared for the next of Hipper's raids. Hipper was disturbed by the fact that heavy British ships always seemed to appear when he was on a raid, but instead of identifying the true reasons – code-breaking and extraordinarily lax German wireless discipline – Hipper thought that the culprits were British fishing boats working on Dogger Bank. They had to be spies, radioing the Admiralty every time his ships passed nearby, so for his next operation Hipper planned to destroy the multitude of fishing boats operating in the area.

## THE BATTLE OF DOGGER BANK

On the evening of 23 January 1915 Hipper put to sea with *Seydlitz*, *Derfflinger*, *Moltke*, *Blücher*, four light cruisers and nineteen destroyers. Admiralty code-breaking was in fine form and the Grand Fleet was made aware of the steaming of Hipper's force without *Von der Tann*, which was in drydock. The British battlecruisers left harbour at 18:00, within an hour of the departure of Hipper. Beatty had *Lion*, *Tiger*, *Princess Royal*, *Indomitable* and *New Zealand*, as well as supporting light cruisers and destroyers, but this was only one element of powerful forces, including the Grand Fleet, set to converge on the Dogger Bank on 24 January. Beatty called action stations at 07:00 even before the Germans were sighted, but twenty minutes later the screening forces clashed. Hipper first thought that there were isolated British light forces in the area, as there was no clue that Beatty's force had left harbour, but soon Hipper realised that he was in a British trap. At 07:35 Hipper's force turned for home, but the maximum speed of his force was restricted to *Blücher*'s 20kts.

Beatty had the edge in speed and quickly closed the gap between the forces, although his own squadron became stretched out as the 'Splendid Cats' gradually left the older *New Zealand* and *Indomitable* behind. At 08:45 *Lion* opened fire on the *Blücher*, which was last in Hipper's column, and she soon became the target of *Princess Royal* and *Tiger* as well. *Blücher* slowed as she absorbed repeated hits of 13.5in shells. The design weakness in *Blücher* was demonstrated when charges and shells using ammunition rails running from the magazines of the aft beam turrets to the forward beam turrets were ignited and a raging fire developed amidships.

By 09:30 *New Zealand* had joined in the firing and Beatty issued an order for each of his ships to fire on its opposite number. *Blücher* had slowed to 17kts and veered out of the column to the northeast because of steering damage, and British fire began to shift to Hipper's flagship, the *Seydlitz*. At 10:01 *Seydlitz* hit *Lion* and knocked out her electrical system, which proved to be one of the pivotal strikes of the battle. Suffering additional hits by German shells, *Lion* had to drop out of the line, so Beatty ordered the *Indomitable* to destroy the enemy breaking away to the north, which was *Blücher*. *Lion* had no electricity for the radio and only two signal halyards intact, so with the signal to attack the rear of the enemy column still on the halyard, Beatty's error-prone Flag Lieutenant raised the squadron signal to turn to the north. The entire British force, not just *Indomitable*, had just been directed to concentrate on *Blücher*.

It is sometimes said that one learns more through defeat than through victory, and this was certainly true at the Battle of

Dogger Bank. Another key hit, this time on *Seydlitz*, happened at 10:40, when a 13.5in shell from *Lion* penetrated the rear face of the barbette of the aftermost 11in gun turret, exploding in the shell-handling chamber underneath and igniting sixty-two charges. A few survivors tried to escape into the shell-handling chamber in the adjacent turret and opened flash-proof doors connecting the two barbettes. The flash explosion travelled through the open doors and ignited the ready ammunition in the next barbette, creating a new pillar of fire. Every man in the aft two turrets was lost but the ship was not, as the aft magazine was flooded before the fire could reach it. The near-loss of *Seydlitz* to the haphazard shell-handling procedures was an eye-opener, providing the German fleet with an important lesson that led to greatly improved anti-flash precautions. The Royal Navy would not learn that same lesson until Jutland.

As Hipper steamed to safety, the *Blücher* was finished off by four battlecruisers, receiving 50 to 200 large calibre hits and two torpedo strikes before rolling over at 12:07. Although he did resume the chase, Beatty soon realised that Hipper had too great a lead and his ships would soon be entering more dangerous waters, too close to the German fleet base. As a consequence of the Battle of Dogger Bank, aggressive actions of the capital ships against the Royal Navy were greatly restricted and the fleet commander, Admiral von Ingenohl, was sacked and replaced by the far more passive Admiral Hugo von Pohl. For the remainder of 1915, there were only two timid sorties that stayed within 100 miles of the German port. In August 1915 *Von der Tann*, *Seydlitz* and *Moltke* were sent to the eastern Baltic as heavy support for operations in the Gulf of Riga against the Russians. On 10 August the trio silenced Russian shore batteries on the island of Utoe at the entrance of the Bay and also took pot shots at a Russian cruiser, which quickly left the area. In addition to the constant threat of mines, British submarines posed the greatest danger to the German heavy ships. On 16 August *Seydlitz* caught the British *E 9* on the surface and opened fire, although the submarine managed to dive before she received a hit. It was the British turn on 19 August, when *E 1* found the German battlecruisers at close range. The *Seydlitz* was very close but the torpedo from *E 1* passed ahead of *Seydlitz* but made a lucky hit on *Moltke*, which took on 1500 tons of water but maintained her operations. After the Riga operation was called off, the trio returned to the North Sea base.

In January 1916 von Pohl, who was terminally ill, was replaced by a much more aggressive officer, Reinhard von Scheer. Scheer decided to revive the policy of coastal attacks designed to trap and destroy a small portion of the British fleet. The first operation was timed to coincide with a Zeppelin attack on British ports on the night of 5/6 March. Although nothing was encountered, Scheer was well into the shipping routes before the British realised the High Seas Fleet was out, because Scheer had maintained wireless silence. On 24 April 1916 the fleet sortied for a raid against Lowestoft but en route *Seydlitz* hit a mine and had to return to port, although the remaining battlecruisers completed their mission, bombarding Lowestoft and Yarmouth without interruption. The next operation, postponed until *Seydlitz* had been repaired, was designed to sweep the Skagerrak and Kattegat and got underway early on 31 May 1916.

## THE BATTLE OF JUTLAND

The Grand Fleet steamed out of Scapa Flow and Beatty's battlecruisers left their separate base at Rosyth on the night of the 30th, before the High Seas Fleet left the next morning. Although the Royal Navy had forewarning of a major operation, it was only educated guesswork that allowed the British to intercept Hipper's force. At 15:28 the British opened fire on German torpedo boats and the greatest naval battle of the First World War had begun. The first portion of the battle has been called the Run to the South, as Hipper tried to lure Beatty south to be destroyed by Scheer's battleships. Hipper had five battlecruisers in column, *Lützow* (flag), *Derfflinger*, *Seydlitz*, *Moltke* and *Von der Tann* against Beatty's six ships: *Lion* (flag), *Princess Royal*, *Queen Mary*, *Tiger*, *New Zealand* and *Indefatigable*. However, Beatty was also supported by four *Queen Elizabeth* class battleships of the 5th Battle Squadron armed with eight 15in guns, although they had become separated.

There were sixty miles between Hipper and Scheer's main fleet and at 16:00 Hipper signalled for each ship to engage its opposite number. Visibility aided Hipper as the sun was to the west, silhouetting Beatty's ships, and although Beatty had an advantage in maximum range of main guns, he chose to close the range rapidly. It was Hipper's ships that opened fire at 16:48. With one ship extra, Beatty intended that two ships fire on *Lützow*, while the remaining four German battlecruisers would receive fire from one ship. *Queen Mary*, which had not received the distribution of fire signal, engaged the *Seydlitz*, third in line, leaving *Derfflinger* unmolested by British fire for ten minutes and allowing her to fire very accurate salvos at her target, the *Princess Royal*. Both *Princess Royal* and *Tiger* had turrets put out of action, but in return *Queen Mary*, always a crack gunnery ship, knocked out 'D' turret of *Seydlitz* when one of her 13.5in shells penetrated the barbette armour at 16:57 and ignited four charges (compared to the sixty-two ignited in a similar hit on the barbette of 'E' turret at the Battle of Dogger Bank). The anti-flash precautions put in place after Dogger Bank contained the damage just to 'D' turret. By contrast, at 17:00 a 12in shell from *Lützow* hit 'Q' amidship turret on *Lion* and if it were not for the bravery of mortally wounded Major F J W Harvey, RM, who ordered the magazine doors closed and magazine flooded, burning charges most likely would have reached the magazine, destroying the ship.

*Von der Tann* and *Indefatigable* had been engaged in a ship-to-ship duel for fifteen minutes when *Indefatigable* was hit aft by two or three 11in shells and then by two more forward with her next salvo. Initially no smoke or flames were observed but after over 30 seconds the *Indefatigable* exploded. The lengthy delay from the hits to the explosion strongly indicates the loss was caused by a lack of proper anti-flash procedures, rather than a direct penetration of a magazine. *Von der Tann* had little time to enjoy her victory because at 17:06 she came under fire from *Barham* of the 5th Battle Squadron, and as the other *Queen Elizabeth* class battleships entered firing range, they concentrated fire on the last two German battlecruisers with two targeting *Von der Tann* and two *Moltke*. Extended range and the tremendous amount of smoke lying between them and their targets meant that the British battleships could only fire intermittently, but both *Von der Tann* and *Moltke* were hit.

By 17:16 *Derfflinger* had shifted fire from *Princess Royal* to *Queen Mary*, which was already engaged by *Seydlitz*. *Queen Mary* was hit by three shells out of a four-shell salvo and nothing seemed to happen until the next salvo arrived at 17:25 when there were two more hits. Again there was nothing initially apparent, other than some black smoke. Suddenly, the *Queen Mary* was enveloped in a massive explosion amidships and forward, as the ship broke in half. As with the *Indefatigable*, the significant delay between the shell hits and magazine blowing up suggests that the explosion was caused by lax anti-flash procedures, rather than penetration of a magazine.

Beatty was still confident: the 5th Battle Squadron had rapidly closed the German battlecruisers and he still foresaw the destruction of Hipper's force. However, at 17:38 the cruiser *Southampton* reported sighting the entire High Seas Fleet deployed in battle column, approaching from the south, confirmed a few minutes later by *Champion*. Beatty ordered a turn to the northwest, towards the Grand Fleet, at 17:43, although it was a quarter of an hour before the 5th Battle Squadron complied. The 'Run to the South' had lasted 58 minutes, during which the German battlecruisers had scored 42 major hits on the British battlecruisers, destroying two of them, and two more hits on battleships of the 5th Battle Squadron. In turn Hipper's ships had been hit 17 times, eleven from the battlecruisers and six from the 5th Battle Squadron. *Von der Tann* and *Seydlitz* each had one turret permanently put out of action and *Lützow* had a large hole on the forecastle, which would eventually play a part in the loss of the ship. Now began the 'Run to the North' during which Hipper and Scheer confidently expected to destroy a significant portion of the British Fleet. But just as Hipper had led Beatty to the High Seas Fleet, Beatty was now leading the entire German fleet to the Grand Fleet. At 17:46 Scheer ordered the leading German battleships to open fire but the range of 21,000 to 22,000yds was still too great.

Hipper had turned his battlecruisers at 17:50 to lead the German battleships, maintaining speed even after *Seydlitz* took a torpedo hit from a British destroyer. However, Hipper's ships were suffering in a fire-fight with the 5th Battle Squadron and Hipper slowed his force to 15kts in order to allow the German battleships to close the gap. At 18:50 Beatty's battlecruisers were sighted by the lead battleship of the Grand Fleet, at a time when Hipper and Scheer were still unaware of its presence. In the van of the Grand Fleet was the 3rd Battlecruiser Squadron, consisting of the three ships of the *Invincible* class, under Rear Admiral Horace Hood, at that time some 25 miles ahead of the battleships. It was another half an hour before Hipper found his ships engaged from two directions with battleships to the north and the 3rd Battlecruiser Squadron to the northeast. Aboard *Derfflinger* the gunnery officer clearly sighted Hood's flagship, HMS *Invincible*, and opened fire. At 19:31 one of *Derfflinger*'s shells struck *Invincible* and in a short span the amidships magazine exploded. However, before her sudden loss, *Invincible* had struck a fatal blow at *Lützow*. One of her 12in shells pierced the forward armoured bulkhead of Hipper's flagship, allowing progressive flooding from the bow to amidships. At 19:33 Scheer ordered his fleet to simultaneously turn south in order to get his ships out of the concentrated gunfire of the Grand Fleet as quickly as possible. *Lützow* was losing speed from the progressive flooding and could no longer keep up with his other ships, so Hipper and his staff left the ship and transferred to the torpedo boat *G 39* a little before 20:00. By 19:50 the British capital ships had lost sight of the German ships and Jellicoe assumed they had all turned south to reach the safety of German ports. He accordingly turned the Grand Fleet to the southeast.

Scheer had made another turn to the east with his battlecruisers, led by *Derfflinger*, to assume the point position ahead of the battleships. This turn put him in a direct collision course with the Grand Fleet. Once the fleets again made contact, the German battlecruisers and lead battleships were soon taking punishment and at 20:13 Scheer ordered his battlecruisers to attack the enemy fleet and five minutes later the battleships again reversed course simultaneously. With the four battlecruisers charging the entire British fleet – *Lützow* was separated and out of action – the battlecruisers were each engaged by a number of ships, *Derfflinger* especially suffering. Nevertheless, the German battlecruisers closed to within 7700yds of the nearest British battleships, but their 'Death Ride' had served its purpose: the High Seas Fleet had disengaged successfully. At 20:20 it was time to extradite the battlecruisers from the overwhelming firepower of the Grand Fleet. In coordination with a massed destroyer torpedo attack, the battlecruisers turned to the west to disengage. For a while they remained unmolested but at 21:18 they were seen by Beatty's battlecruisers at a range of 8500yds with *Derfflinger* and *Seydlitz* receiving heavy punishment. The German ships turned further to the west to get out of British fire.

With the heavy smoke and steadily failing light conditions of twilight, the firing ceased but Scheer was in a predicament, with the Grand Fleet blocking the direct line to the German ports. The *Derfflinger* and *Von der Tann*, whose top speed had been reduced to 18kts, fell in behind the German battleships. As the night progressed *Seydlitz* and *Moltke* separated and each ship briefly encountered British battleships at very close ranges, but they were not engaged. Scheer turned his fleet to the east and passed behind the Grand Fleet in the darkness. At midnight the lone *Lützow* was steaming south at 7kts, still hoping to reach safety, but the flooding increased inexorably and at 02:20 the ship was abandoned; at 02:45 two German torpedoes finished her off.

At dawn Jellicoe, who believed the High Seas Fleet was still to his west saw nothing and ordered the Grand Fleet to turn north, further increasing the distance between his fleet and the High Seas Fleet to the east. The Battle of Jutland was over and the German battlecruisers had proved their qualities of survivability. *Seydlitz* was close to sinking but was eventually towed to safety, and all four of the surviving battlecruisers required more time to repair than any of the damaged German battleships. Repairs to *Moltke* were completed on 30 July with *Von der Tann* completing three days later on 2 August; the heavily damaged *Seydlitz* and *Derfflinger* took until 16 September and 15 October respectively. This was the last significant engagement of the German battlecruisers.

In October 1917 *Moltke* was detached to become the fleet flagship for Operation Albion, a successful large-scale amphibious operation to seize a series of islands to the north of the Gulf of Riga, to cut the Russian army's supply route to Riga itself. During the action on 12 October *Moltke* was targeted by a coastal artillery battery consisting of 12in guns on the island of Osel, but was not hit. This ended her active involvement in the operation. The last major operation of the battlecruisers of the Scouting Group was a sweep up to Norway on 23 April 1918 to catch British convoys. The Grand Fleet sortied but never got to within 100 miles of the German ships. *Moltke* suffered a machinery failure and for a time was reduced to a top speed of 4kts, being towed by the battleship *Oldenburg*. The tow was later cast off and *Moltke* was proceeding

**Above:** *Moltke* leading the surviving battlecruisers home on the morning after Jutland. The ship is down by the stern having shipped 1000 tons of water, but was the least badly damaged of the 1st Scouting Group and at this stage was still capable of 25kts. During the previous night Hipper had transferred his flag to the ship from the stricken *Lützow*. *(Bundesarchiv 134-B4002)*

**Left:** *Seydlitz* was severely damaged during the Battle of Jutland, taking twenty-six heavy shell hits as well as a torpedo strike forward. Only the most heroic efforts by the crew kept the ship afloat, eventually with more than 5000 tons of water in the hull. This view of the ship in dock at Wilhelmshaven gives some idea of the scale of the damage suffered, and ship was not declared seaworthy again until 2 October. *(©National Maritime Museum L5848)*

under her own power when she was struck by a torpedo from the British submarine *E 42* and took on 1800 tons of water. She reached port without further mishap.

At the Armistice, all of the battlecruisers were interned at Scapa Flow, where they swung at anchor until all were scuttled on their commander's orders on 21 June 1919.

## SMS *GOEBEN*

The *Goeben* lived a different life, and the longest life of any battlecruiser ever built. Launched on 7 April 1910, the ship had been afloat for over six decades when she was scrapped in 1971. Her separation from the other battlecruisers resulted from Kaiser Wilhelm's desire to have a German naval presence in the Mediterranean, the *Goeben* and light cruiser *Breslau* being dispatched in 1912 under the command of Rear Admiral Wilhelm Souchon. His force was at Pola, then an Austrian port, replacing her boiler tubes as the events leading inexorably to the First World War unfolded. Souchon was anxious not to be bottled up with the Austrian Fleet if war broke out with Britain and France, so on 29 July he headed south in order to clear the Adriatic.

On station the British had three battlecruisers, *Inflexible*, *Indomitable* and *Indefatigable*, and four armoured cruisers under the command of Rear Admiral Berkeley Milne, whose prime mission was to find *Goeben*. Milne was ordered to prevent the *Goeben* from leaving the Adriatic but Souchon had already cleared the area before Milne received the order. *Goeben* was reported at the Italian port of Taranto and Milne was ordered to send two of his battlecruisers to Gibraltar to prevent a break out into the Atlantic. These ships, *Indefatigable* and *Indomitable*, sighted *Goeben* on 4 August, shortly after the German ships had received a message to steam east to Constantinople. Since Great Britain was not yet at war, they started shadowing *Goeben*, waiting for the British ultimatum to Germany to expire at midnight. For six hours the British battlecruisers were in contact with *Goeben* but Souchon had his stokers endure extraordinary heat to keep the boilers at maximum pressure to squeeze every knot out the *Goeben*'s machinery. Finally the *Goeben* broke contact. At 01:15 on 5 August Milne was radioed that Great Britain and Germany were now at war. Shortly thereafter he learned that Souchon was at Messina. He stationed his ships west of Sicily to block the German ships from intercepting French troop convoys in the Western Mediterranean, but Souchon turned east. He did not know how great a distance separated *Goeben* from the British battlecruisers and was still steaming as fast as the *Goeben* was capable; four stokers died of heat stroke and the result of a boiler-tube explosion. The British never came close to regaining contact. By the evening of 10 August *Goeben* was passing the Dardanelles on the way to Constantinople.

The German government offered Turkey the *Goeben* and *Breslau* as a gift, and on 16 August 1914 both ships were transferred to Turkey, being renamed *Yavuz Sultan Selim* and *Midilli*, although Souchon and his crews still manned the ships. For two months *Goeben* was inactive as Souchon took the time to repair his over-worked machinery. Turkey was still neutral but in October the Turks decide on a pre-emptive strike, and *Goeben* bombarded the Russian port of Sevastopol on 29 October, firing forty-seven 11in and twelve 5.9in rounds at the anchored Russian Black Seas fleet; in turn her aft funnel was hit by two 12in shells, which killed 14 of *Goeben*'s crew. On 1 November Turkey formally declared war as an ally of Germany and Austro-Hungary.

For the remainder of 1914 *Goeben* and *Breslau* were employed in the Black Sea. On 18 November there was a very short engagement in heavy mist with five Russian pre-dreadnought battleships at a range of four miles. *Goeben* fired nineteen 11in rounds, hitting the battleship *Ivstafi* four times. In turn *Goeben* was hit by one 12in shell, which knocked out one of the 5.9in guns. On 26 December she struck two mines, but made it to port under her own power. However, Turkey did not have a dry-dock capable of taking *Goeben* and lacked skilled shipwrights. Workers had to be brought in

**Below:** *Moltke* saw more action after Jutland than the rest of the battlecruisers, acting as flagship for Operation Albion in the Baltic and later surviving a torpedo hit from a British submarine in April 1918, repairs to the latter taking until September. She is seen here at the end of the war. *(©National Maritime Museum N11737)*

**Left:** *Goeben* leaving Wilhelmshaven in November 1912 on her Mediterranean deployment. As it transpired, the ship would never see Germany again.

from Germany, and a cofferdam blister was built over the holes, repairs taking until 13 April 1915. The Gallipoli landings began on 25 April and *Goeben* moved south to bombard the allied troops. In an early example of aerial directed naval gunfire, on 27 April *Goeben* was engaged by the 15in guns of HMS *Queen Elizabeth*, directed by the observer from a kite balloon. *Goeben* quickly moved behind a cliff to get out of the firing line. A similar occurrence on 30 April involved five 12in shells from HMS *Lord Nelson* landing close to the battlecruiser before she again reached the shelter of the cliff. In early May she was once more in the Black Sea, and during another encounter with the battleships of the Russian fleet *Goeben* hit the *Tri Sviatitelia* and *Ioan Zlatoust* and was hit by three 12in shells in return. For the balance of 1915 *Goeben* stayed in Turkish waters, primarily due to a coal shortage.

The new year of 1916 found a new antagonist for *Goeben* as the Russian Black Sea dreadnoughts were completed. She had encounters with *Imperatritsa Ekaterina II* in January 1916 and *Imperatritsa Maria* in September. Another new opponent was aerial attack in which *Goeben* was the target of night bombing on April 14 and July 7. The *Goeben* was fairly inactive in 1917, covering Turkish landings in June and was hit by a bomb at Constantinople on 9 July 1917. Early in 1918 it was decided to make a surprise attack on the warships and transports in the harbour of the island of Mudros. *Goeben*, *Breslau* and four destroyers departed Constantinople on 19 January 1918 and were in the Aegean Sea the next day. Although *Goeben* hit a mine at 06:10, damage was minor and she reached Mudros at 07:40 where the British monitors *Raglan* and *M 28* were quickly sunk. *Breslau* hit a mine at 08:30 and as *Goeben* tried to take her in tow *Goeben* hit a mine and *Breslau* detonated four more mines and sank. By 09:00 *Goeben* was under air attack and while retiring struck a third mine at 09:48. She then ran aground and was stationary for the next six days. From the afternoon of 20 January until the 25th *Goeben* was under continuous aerial attack. The bombs ranged from 25lb to 112lb, but there were also 9.2in shells converted to bombs used against her. In total there were 65 attacks dropping 180 bombs. Indirect monitor fire was also used against the stationary ship. During all of this *Goeben* was only hit by two small bombs, which did minor damage. Finally, it took an old Turkish battleship, along with the tugs to extricate the *Goeben* on 26

**Left:** *Goeben* famously escaped from the pursuing British squadron on the outbreak of war by dint of steaming at her maximum sustained speed of 24kts for half a day. The effort cost the lives of four stokers from heat exhaustion and burns resulting from a boiler tube explosion. After the ship arrived at Constantinople, boiler repairs took two months to complete, although the ship was able to steam during that time. *(Bundesarchiv 134-B0032)*

## BATTLE DAMAGE HISTORY

| Ship | Date | Type | Seriousness | Repair Time |
|---|---|---|---|---|
| *Blücher* | 24.1.1915 | 50-200 shell hits, 2 torpedo hits | Sunk | N/A |
| *Von der Tann* | 31.5.1916 | 4 heavy shell hits | Minor | 2 months |
| *Moltke* | 16.8.1915 | 1 torpedo | Minor | 1 month |
| | 31.5.1916 | 4 heavy shell hits | Minor | 2 months |
| | 23.4.1918 | 1 torpedo | Minor | 1 month |
| *Goeben* | 29.10.1914 | Two 12in | Minor | 1 week |
| | 18.11.1914 | One 12in | Minor | 2 weeks |
| | 26.12.1914 | mine | Heavy | 3 months |
| | 10.5.1915 | Two 12in | Moderate | 1 month |
| | 9.7.1917 | Aircraft bomb | Minor | 1 month |
| | 20.1.1918 | 3 mines, bomb splinter damage | Heavy | 2 months |
| *Seydlitz* | 24.1.1915 | Two 13.5in | Almost fatal | 3 months |
| | 24.4.1916 | mine | Minor | 1 month |
| | 31.5.1916 | 21 heavy, 2 medium shell hits, 1 torpedo | Almost fatal | 5 months |
| *Derfflinger* | 24.1.1915 | One 13.5in | Minor | 1 month |
| | 31.5.1916 | 17 heavy, 9 medium shell hits | Moderate | 5 months |
| *Lützow* | 31.5.1916 | 24 heavy shell hits | Sunk | N/A |

January and she reached Constantinople the following day. The cofferdam used in 1915 was again employed to repair the mine damage.

With the war coming to an end the German personnel were replaced with a Turkish crew on 2 November 1918. Under the original peace treaty, *Goeben* was to be surrendered to Great Britain for scrapping, but a Turkish civil war erupted in which the sultan was removed and a republic declared. A new treaty allowed Turkey to retain the ship, which was unserviceable and so extensively damaged that even the Turks thought of scrapping her. Eventually a dry-dock of sufficient size was built and from 1928 to 1930 *Goeben* was repaired. Her official name had been shortened to *Yavuz Selim* and in 1936 was further shortened to just *Yavuz*. She served in training and ceremonial duties, including a visit to Malta in 1936. *Yavuz* was placed in reserve in 1948 and remained in that capacity for the next two decades. In 1970 there were tentative negotiations with Germany to bring her home as a museum commemorating the German Navy. These fell through and in 1971 *Yavuz*, nee *Goeben*, was scrapped, closing the book on the impressive history of German battlecruisers.

**Below:** During the war *Goeben* was based at the port of Stenia (modern Istinye), above Istanbul on the European shore of the Bosporus, roughly halfway between the Black Sea and the Mediterranean. This view of the ship alongside at Stenia is undated, but must predate May 1915 when No 4 5.9in gun was removed from each broadside. *(Bundesarchiv 134-B0025)*

# Model Products

As detailed in this book, Imperial Germany commissioned just seven battlecruisers; adding the armoured cruiser *Blücher* which operated with the First Scouting Group and the never-completed *Mackensen* and *Ersatz Yorck* brings the total to ten. Given this small number, and the widespread interest in the ships, it is not surprising that all of them are available in kit form. Kits in white metal, paper, and resin have long been available and they are now offered in injection moulded plastic with the release of *Derfflinger* and *Lützow* from Flyhawk Models. The most common commercial scales of 1:1250, 1:700, 1:350, and 1:250 are well represented with kits available in all those scales.

No one resin manufacturer dominates the market, with multiple kits available from HP, Combrig, NNT, and WSW. The quality of resin castings varies between manufacturers and sometimes even between kits from the same manufacturer. Most require some form of clean-up along the waterline and need careful attention to casting flaws such as pinholes, warping, and rough edges.

In general the kits from HP have the lightest amount of moulded-in detail, while the latest releases from Combrig, NNT, and WSW approach the levels of detail normally found in slide-moulded injected plastic kits. However, all the resin kits reviewed in this section will build into quality models, dependent only on the modeller's skill level and amount of super-detailing applied.

## NAVIS/NEPTUN ALL CLASSES — 1:1250 Scale

This German company is well renowned for its exquisite set of white metal models with literally hundreds of ships in the range. They produce models of all the battlecruisers as well as *Blücher* and the never-completed *Mackensen* and *Ersatz Yorck*. *Derfflinger* is available in both pre- and post-Jutland fits. The kits come fully assembled and are painted an overall light grey with some black highlights. There are enhanced versions available for the seven battlecruisers that actually entered service, complete with rigging and additional painted details mounted on a wood base with a plastic case.

**Left:** Navis Neptun model of *Blücher* (Kit 30N); **right:** The Navis Neptun detailed and rigged model of *Lützow* (Kit 23V), with wooden base and clear plastic case. *(Photos courtesy of Navis-Neptun)*

## COMBRIG *BLÜCHER* — 1:700 Scale

Combrig has a well-deserved reputation for accuracy and fine detail and this kit is certainly no exception. It perfectly captures the lines and busy deck layout of the ill-fated armoured cruiser and scales out at precisely 530 feet. The resin cast hull is complete up to the main deck and the four main superstructure pieces fit nicely into cut-outs on the main deck. There is plenty of detail on the decks and the armour belt and casemates are clearly defined. There are many smaller parts with anchors, ventilators, searchlights, and ship's boats cast on separate resin sprues.

*Blücher*'s main gun turrets were not identical and the kit pieces accurately reflect the differences; gun barrels are separate. *Blücher* had an intricate boat deck around her after funnel and this is represented in finely detailed resin with photo-etch pieces. The one-piece funnels have plenty of cast-on detail and are hollow at the top which will provide depth when the photo-etch grilles are applied. The compre-

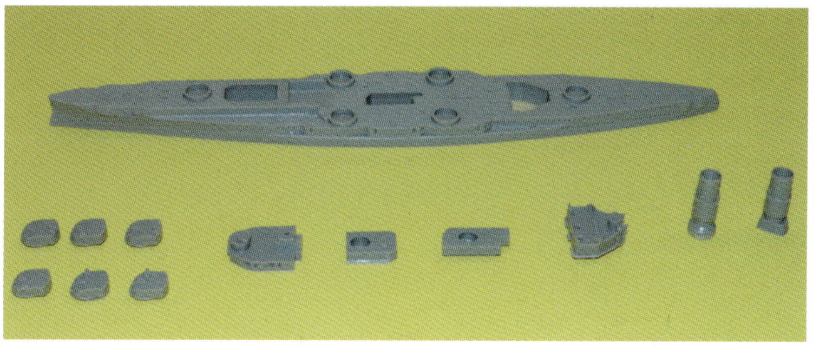

The hull and main components of the Combrig *Blücher*. The cut-outs for the main superstructure pieces are clearly evident.

Box art for the Combrig *Blücher*

hensive photo-etch sheet also contains lattice work for the very distinctive amidships boat cranes, ladders, anchor chain, parts for the boats and the torpedo net shelves, but not the nets themselves. Two instruction sheets include a profile and plan view showing rigging details and another outlining the major part assembly on one side and placement of boats on the other. There are no painting instructions.

■ Review kit kindly lent by **Leonard Fricke**

## WSW *BLÜCHER* 1:700 Scale

The casting quality of this kit is exceptional. The main hull is complete up to the superstructure deck and nicely captures the complex shapes of the decks and hull, scaling out perfectly to the actual length of 530 feet. The forward and after superstructures, the main turret barbettes, and the base of the after funnel are cast in place, with very delicate bulwarks around the edges of the bridge and after superstructure. The deck planking is represented by very finely scribed lines and there is an adequate amount of detailing in the form of bollards, skylights, hatches, anchor chains, the torpedo nets and anchors.

The smaller parts such as boats and searchlights are cast on resin sprues, and there is a lot of finely cast lattice work for the searchlight platforms. The one-piece funnels are hollowed out and have some cast-on detail. The three different types of main armament turrets are provided, with very fine gun barrels already in place. The casemate gun barrels will need to be supplied from plastic rod; the length is provided in the instructions. The four 8.8cm guns are cast as one piece with shields and gun barrels. Pins are already in place to support the boat deck around the after funnel. Finely cast resin masts are included along with the distinctive amidships cranes. There are two instruction sheets, one with a profile and plan view showing rigging details, boat and main armament placement, painting instructions, and a parts list. The other sheet has exploded views for assembly of the superstructure. Yardarms for both masts and supports for the forward tripod will need to be supplied from plastic rod and/or wire using the very clear dimensions in the instructions.

Casting all the major components as one piece means that this kit will not require much effort to complete. However, for more experienced modellers there are a couple of areas that will require attention. The forward rake of the bow is a little too pronounced, so will need correction with sandpaper. The casemates at the very stern of the ship project out too much; they need to be removed and sanded to the right depth before being reattached. Despite these shortcomings, this will make a fine model right from the box.

**Right:** Box art for the WSW *Blücher*

**Below:** Detail view showing how the amidships boat deck fits into place

■ Review kits kindly lent by **Pavel Vacata** of **Admiralty Model Works** and courtesy of **Thomas Weihs** at **WSW-Modellbau**

## HP *VON DER TANN* 1:700 Scale

The first of the German battlecruisers is well represented with this kit. The one-piece resin hull is complete up to the main deck and nicely captures the complex shapes near the bow with the raised forecastle deck and casemates. The scale length is bang on the actual length of 562 feet. The amidships casemates and the embrasures on the stern quarters are also done very well. The deck features a moderate level of detail with bollards, anchors and chains, and some hatches, planking being represented with thinly scribed lines. The after superstructure, funnels, and bridge platforms are separeately cast on thin resin wafers, with some added detailing of pipes and ventilators. The main gun turrets are correctly shaped and feature some detail on their roofs. The boats are adequate but not to the standards of those found in Combrig kits, and the two-piece funnels do not feature any grilles.

My example came with brass turned barrels for the main armament, which is an improvement on the overly-thick resin barrels supplied. The casemate gun barrels will need to be cut from plastic rod, but the AA gun mounts are included. There are no torpedo net shelves and booms, and the masts and cranes will have to be scratch-built using additional reference as the two assembly instruction sheets do not include scale dimensions, although they will prove useful when placing the ship's boats. A small sheet of flags is also included. This kit will build up into a nice replica of the real ship right out of the box, but more experienced modellers will find plenty of scope for detailing.

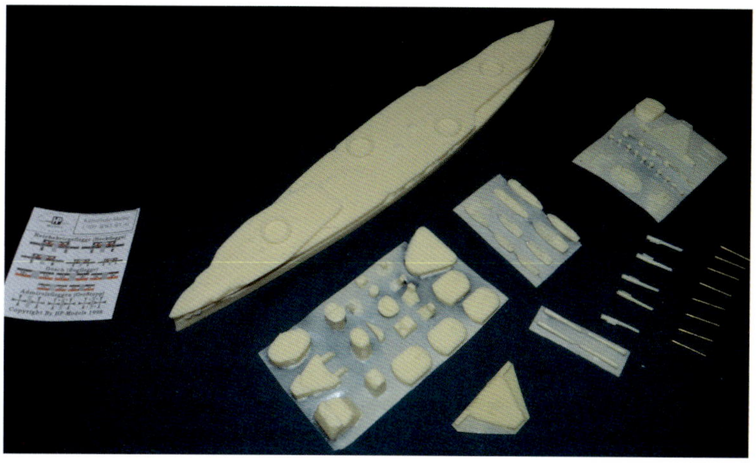

**Above:** Components of the HP *Von der Tann* kit

**Left:** Box art of the HP *Von der Tann* kit

■ Review kit kindly lent by **Roger Torgeson**

## HP *MOLTKE* 1913

1:700 Scale

The main hull casting has the superstructure blocks and the bases of the funnels already cast in place. There are plenty of cast-in air intakes, and the main armour belt and the open casemates are well defined. The asymmetrical positioning of the casemates, port and starboard, is captured as well. The deck has an adequate amount of detail with bollards, hatches, breakwaters, and boat chocks on finely scribed deck planking. The casting is very crisp but scales out some 9 feet shorter than the actual length of 610 feet. The remaining superstructure parts along with the upper funnels, searchlights, and anchors are found on resin wafers or attached to resin blocks. Metal anchor chain is supplied as well. Both funnels have hollow caps, but no grilles are supplied.

The boats are the ones common to the HP *Goeben*, *Moltke*, and *Seydlitz* kits and are well shaped and detailed, easily positioned with the aid of cast-in boat chocks. The main gun turrets, with turned brass barrels, are correctly shaped and have some detail on the roofs. The casemate and AA guns are cast as single pieces complete with gun barrels. The cranes are cast in one piece on a resin wafer, and the lower masts are cast in white metal. Torpedo net shelves and booms are not included. The three instruction sheets include templates for building the masts and boat davits, with straightforward directions for building the masts from wire and the white metal pieces. A small sheet of flags is also included.

This kit will build up into a nice model right from the box, with more experienced modellers finding plenty of scope for detailing.

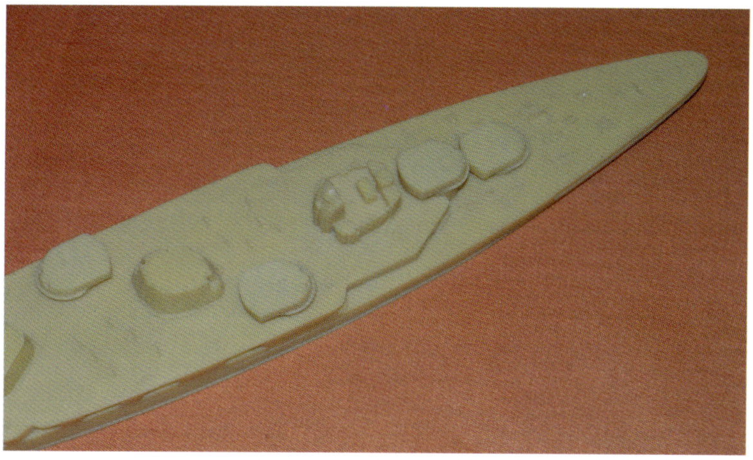

**Above:** Hull casting of HP *Moltke* with main turrets in place

**Left:** Box art of the HP *Moltke*

## HP *GOEBEN* 1914

1:700 Scale

As built, *Goeben* and her sister *Moltke* were virtually identical and HP takes advantage of that fact by providing the same basic kit for both ships, although each includes unique parts that reflect the slight differences between the two sisters. HP provides the differently shaped fore

**Left:** Box art for the HP *Goeben*

**Right:** Components included with the kit

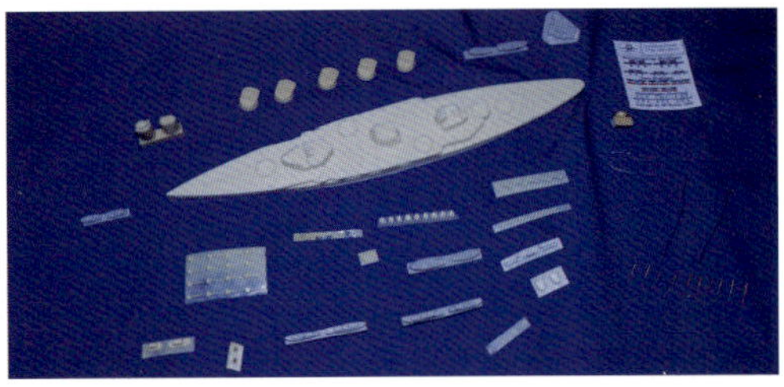

funnel platforms for *Goeben* and leaves out the after funnel cap not fitted in that ship. There are no cranes provided, so the modeller will need to scratch-build them using the dimensions found in the instructions. With the exception of these differences, all comments from the *Moltke* kit apply to this kit as well.

## CLASSIC WARSHIPS SMS *SEYDLITZ* 1:700 Scale

Classic Warships were among the first manufacturers to make resin warships available for sale to the general public. Their kits were very much for experienced modellers with many parts to be scratch-built, but they were quite eye-opening for their time. Long out of production, the overall quality of the castings still holds up well alongside newer offerings and they can still be found online and on the vendor's tables at model shows.

As the crisply cast one-piece hull is complete with both funnels and the fore and aft superstructures, very little will have to be added. There is a moderate level of detail on the decks, with finely inscribed lines for planking and numerous hatches and bollards. The funnels have cast-in air intakes and piping, while the hollowed-out tops will show well if any grillework is added. The main gun turrets, gun barrels, boats, and searchlights are all cast in white metal with surprisingly good detail, especially the boats. The various platforms for the superstructure parts are cast on a thin resin wafer. No anchors or anchor chain is included, and there are no torpedo net shelves or booms. Masts, gun directors, platform bracing, davits, chocks for the boats, and crane booms will have to be built from plastic rod or wire.

There are two instruction sheets, one showing plan and profile views with very comprehensive instructions and specific measurements for each scratch-built piece. However, there is no exploded view showing parts placement.

**Below:** Components of the Classic Warships *Seydlitz* kit

## HP *SEYDLITZ* 1:700 Scale

**Right:** Box art of the HP *Seydlitz* kit

This kit of the much battered German battlecruiser consists of a one-piece hull that has the superstructure and the bases of the two funnels already cast in place. There are some finely cast details present in the form of air intakes, the main armour belt, and the open casemates ready for placing the gun mounts, while the deck also has an adequate amount of detail, including finely scribed planking. The casting is very crisp, but scales out slightly undersized at 645 feet instead of 656.

The few remaining superstructure parts along with searchlights and anchors are found on resin wafers or attached to resin blocks. Metal anchor chain is supplied as well. The top of the fore funnel has a hollow cap; the after funnel top will need to be drilled out if grilles are to be attached. The boats are common to the *Goeben*, *Moltke* and *Seydlitz* kits, but are a step above the usual HP fare. The steam launches are particularly nice with funnels and hollowed-out cockpits. The main gun turrets have some detail on the roofs and they fit nicely into the barbettes cast on the main deck; their gun barrels are turned brass. The casemate and AA guns are cast as single pieces complete with gun barrels. The crane posts are supplied in white metal, but the booms will have to be scratch-built using the dimensions found in the instructions. The lower masts are cast in resin. There are no torpedo net shelves or booms.

There are three instruction sheets, one with an exploded view showing parts assembly, another with a plan and profile, and a third with a parts list. A small sheet of flags is also included. The instructions for building the masts from wire and the resin pieces are very straightforward.

**Below:** Close up of main hull casting showing deck details

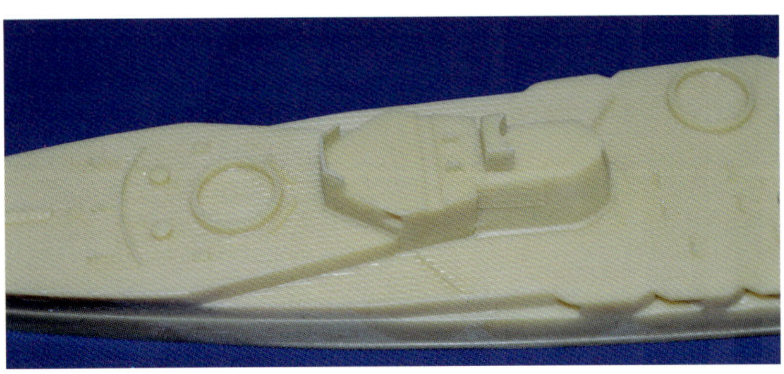

## WSW *SEYDLITZ* 1:700 Scale

WSW provides another fine casting featuring plenty of delicate moulded-in detail. The main hull is cast complete up to the superstructure deck with the main armament barbettes, funnels, and crane posts already in place. There is some bulkhead detail, the air vents are well defined, with anchor chains, boat chocks and other vents also moulded in place. The moulded-in breakwaters and bridge bulwarks are remarkably thin. The torpedo nets are already in place atop very finely cast net shelves and the anchors have also been attached to the hull sides, but the modeller will have to supply the torpedo net booms.

The deck planking is represented by very finely scribed lines and there is an adequate amount of detailing in the form of bollards, skylights, and hatches. The funnels have plenty of detail in the form of handrails and piping. There are no funnel grilles supplied with the kit, but the funnel tops are hollow which will provide depth if they are added. Due to the remarkable amount of cast-in detail there are not a lot of extra parts for this kit, but they are all very crisply moulded with well-defined edges and surface details. The various superstructure platforms are on a single resin wafer, with the boats and searchlights on their own resin sprues. The boats themselves are adequate with funnels and thwarts well defined. The hull lines for the steam launches are too fine at the bows which make them appear a bit 'toy-like'; they could be replaced from the spares box. The main gun turrets have some detail and come with very fine gun barrels already in place. The barrels for the secondary armament are on a resin sprue; the 8.8cm guns consist of a separate gun mount and an open backed shield. Crane booms, masts, and yardarms are very delicately cast and will be quite adequate.

There are two instruction sheets, one with a profile and plan view showing rigging details, painting instructions, and a parts list. The other has photographs on both sides showing parts assembly. Overall this is a very good kit, scaling out perfectly to the actual length of 656 feet, and will build into a fine model right from the box.

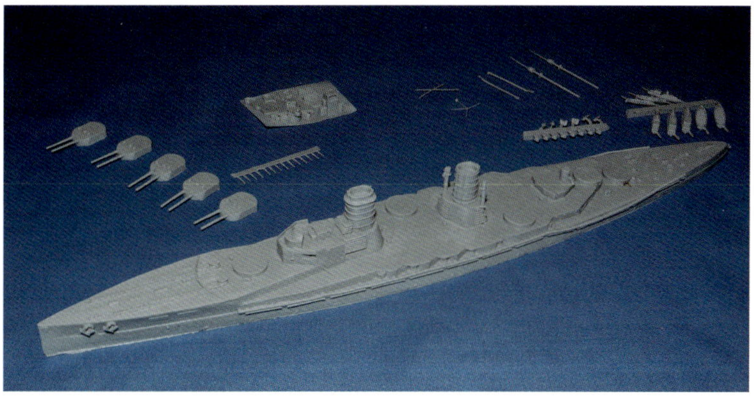

**Above:** Components of the WSW *Seydlitz* kit

Review kit courtesy of **Thomas Weihs** at **WSW-Modellbau**

## COMBRIG *SEYDLITZ* 1:350 Scale

Everything about this kit is stupendous, and not just due to its very large size. The quality of the castings is superb, approaching the fine detail found in new injection-moulded plastic kits, with none of the pitting and hollowing that can be found on some resin kits. The upper and lower hull halves are hollow – so extremely lightweight – and there is plenty of detail on both pieces, from the torpedo tube doors to the well-defined skylights, hatch covers, and coaling ports. The upper hull is cast up to the level of the main deck, including the raised forecastle, with casemate openings and the armour belt well defined, and finely scribed deck planks. The lower hull has the four propeller shaft skegs already cast in place, with the rudders and propellers separately cast.

Because of the ship's very simple superstructure, there are not many pieces that will need to be added to the model; the five main pieces fit nicely into well-defined areas on the main deck, with the rest of the superstructure pieces on a resin wafer. The main gun turrets, with separate barrels, have fine detail on their roofs and rear faces and also fit neatly into their barbettes. The light armament has separate shields and

**Left:** Box art of the Combrig *Seydlitz*

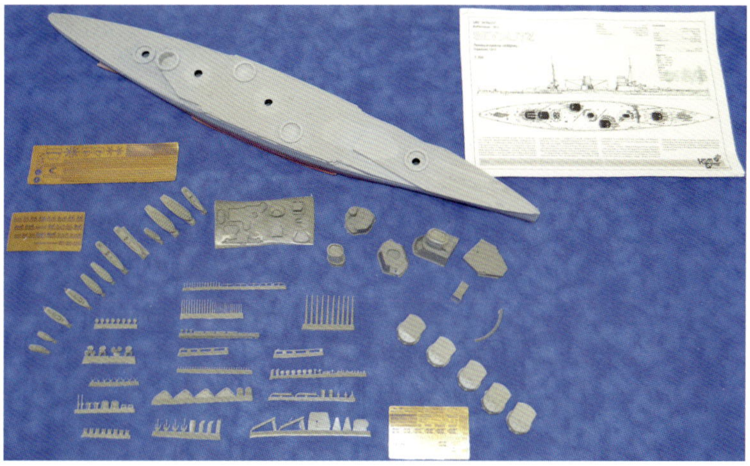

**Below:** Components of the Combrig *Seydlitz* kit

barrels, with different shields for the surface guns carried from 1913 to 1915 and the AA guns carried from 1915 to 1919. The forward funnel is one piece, the after funnel consists of two, but the tops of both are hollow and invite the addition of photo-etch grilles. Masts are supplied in resin.

The ship's boats are nothing short of spectacular: well shaped and moulded, they feature scribed decking and hollowed-out cockpits and engine compartments. However, they have to be positioned by reference to the plan view. Three photo-etch sheets include ladders, torpedo net shelves, superstructure windows, boat rudders and chocks, the heraldic bow shield, crane pieces, after breakwater, and anchor chain. There are no railings, torpedo nets or booms; the modeller will need to create these items. There are four instruction sheets, two with exploded views for parts assembly, a parts list, and a profile and plan drawing. There is also a masking sheet for painting the turret recognition circles.

Available in both waterline and full-hull versions, this is a remarkable kit that will build into a very impressive model.

■ Review kit kindly lent by **Roger Torgeson**

## WSW *DERFFLINGER* 1:700 Scale

This kit depicts *Derfflinger* as she would have appeared going into action at Jutland in 1916, and scales out slightly oversize at about 10 feet longer than the actual 690 feet. The casting is complete up to the upper superstructure deck and funnel bases. The decks are studded with detail: bollards, hatches, boat chocks, anchor chains, and finely scribed deck planking. There is some bulkhead detail, the armour belt, portholes, vents and casemate mountings are well defined. The torpedo net shelves are very delicately cast with the torpedo nets in place, but the booms will have to be supplied by the modeller. The anchors are already in place on the hull as well.

Funnel handrails and piping are present, but the modeller may wish to replace the moulded-on ladders with some from photo-etch. The funnels themselves are hollow at the top, but the kit does not supply photo-etch grilles. The few superstructure parts, searchlight platforms and lattice supports are cast on a thin wafer. The bulwarks for these pieces are remarkably thin. The boats, searchlights, crane booms, crane posts, and davits are on resin sprues. The large davits characteristic of this class incorporate very fine lattice detail. The open boats are well rendered, with the steam launches well detailed but perhaps a little too fine at the bow. The main armament turrets have some detail and feature very thinly cast gun barrels already attached. The secondary armament gun barrels are on a resin sprue; the 8.8cm guns are cast as one piece with open backs to the shields.The masts and yardarms are very delicately cast; the upper yardarms will have to be supplied by the modeller.

There are three instruction sheets: a parts list with painting details, a plan and profile view showing boat placement, and an exploded view showing parts assembly. The casting is very well executed, featuring extremely sharp lines and some very delicate components. Due to the very small number of parts it will assemble very easily into a fine model.

**Below:** Components of the WSW *Derfflinger* kit

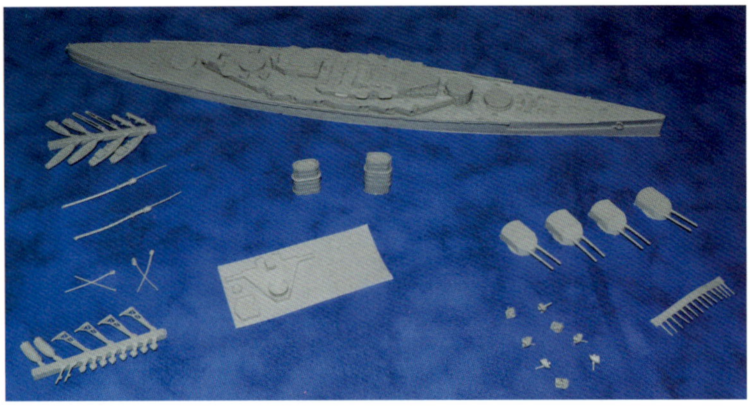

■ Review kit courtesy of **Thomas Weihs** at **WSW-Modellbau**

## FLYHAWK **SMS *DERFFLINGER*** 1916 1:700 Scale

Flyhawk is a relatively new company (2012) which has produced several fine kits of Second World War U-boats in 1:700 scale. *Derfflinger* marks their first foray into surface vessels, and it is an impressive debut. Depicting *Derfflinger* in 1916 at Jutland, this is a very high quality kit that scales out perfectly to 690 feet.

The box is full to the brim with parts – five sprues in all, with separate large pieces for the superstructure. The hull is made up of four pieces: port and starboard sides, the main deck, hull plate, with a weight to give the hull some 'heft'. There is plenty of detailing throughout; the main deck with individual planks and plenty of raised fittings, the hull sides with the raised armour belt and net shelf for the torpedo nets, the funnels with a non-solid moulded-in funnel grille. The main, secondary, and anti-aircraft armament all have separate barrels and gun mounts.

**Right:** Box art for the Flyhawk *Derfflinger*

A photo-etch sheet contains boat cranes to replace the plastic pieces, pre-cut railings, ladders, companionways, jackstays, and details for the rear of the main turrets. A decal sheet has flags, ensigns, bow shield, name plates, and turret recognition circles. The instructions consist of one large folded sheet in full colour on glossy paper. The colour is used to good advantage with colour-coded sections showing where to place all the smaller details such as boats, searchlights, AA armament, deck fittings, photo-etch ladders, torpedo net booms, and railings. There is also a full colour painting and marking guide with references to the Mr Hobby, Tamiya, and WEM Colourcoats ranges.

The attention to detail and the large part count will ensure that this kit will build into a very impressive model. The special edition version of the kit comes with 8 brass barrels for the main armament and a Friedrichshafen FF.33 seaplane.

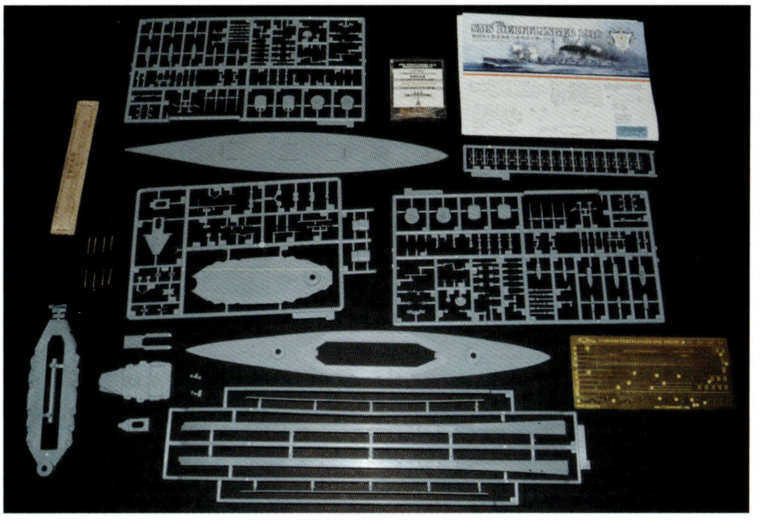

**Above:** The impressive number of parts included with the kit

## HMV *SMS DERFFLINGER* 1:250 Scale

An appealing feature of card models is that no painting is required, the parts being supplied on pre-printed sheets in the finished colours. Offsetting that advantage is the skill set required to cut out the parts accurately and to fold all the components together, sometimes into very complex shapes. This card model comes in the form of a book containing 34 printed sheets. Rated as 'very difficult' by the manufacturer, it is not for the beginner or the faint of heart! There are 2584 parts that will assemble into an impressive 33-inch long model representing *Derfflinger* in her post-Jutland fit with the tripod mainmast. The kit can be assembled with or without the lower hull. A separate set of laser-cut parts for some of the more intricate pieces is also available.

HMV also makes a waterline kit of *Von der Tann* in the same scale. With 2401 parts, the 27-inch long model is rated 'difficult'.

■ Review kit kindly lent by **Kerry Jang**

**Left:** The 1:250 kit of *Derfflinger* from HMV. Despite being labelled '1914', the kit actually depicts *Derfflinger* as she appeared after Jutland with a tripod mast.

**Note:** For photographs of the completed model, see pages 42-3 for the *Derfflinger* kit and pages 28-9 for *Von der Tann*

## WSW *LÜTZOW* 1:700 Scale

Despite being members of the same class, there were detail differences between *Derfflinger* and *Lützow*. In *Lützow* the forward superstructure extended aft around the base of the fore funnel and the bridge decks were of a different shape; she also had an extra bridge deck and two more casemate mounts for the secondary armament. Her fore funnel was fully jacketed and the funnel searchlight platforms differed from those on *Derfflinger*. These details are all fully captured in this kit. With the exception of these differences, all comments from the *Derfflinger* kit apply to this kit as well.

■ Review kit courtesy of **Thomas Weihs** at **WSW-Modellbau**

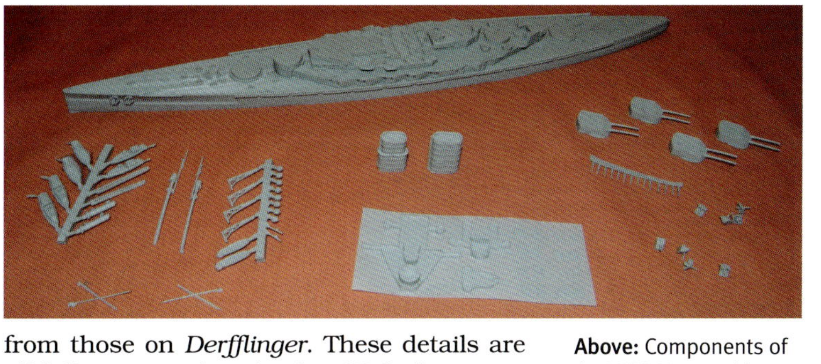

**Above:** Components of the WSW *Lützow* kit

**Left:** Detail view amidships with funnels and main gun turrets in place

## FLYHAWK ***SMS LÜTZOW*** 1916 — 1:700 Scale

Right: The very dramatic box art of the Flyhawk *Lützow*

*Lützow* is the second of Flyhawk's German battlecruisers. This is not a simple re-boxing of the *Derfflinger* kit, but is a brand new tooling with plenty of attention paid to the detail differences between the two sisters. There are three sprues containing parts common to both ships and one new sprue specific to *Lützow*. The basic format is the same as for *Derfflinger* with a four-piece hull and the same level of detail. The main deck and superstructure parts are new to incorporate the extra pair of casemate-mounted 15cm guns.

The photo-etch sheet has extra superstructure parts and searchlight towers in addition to all the parts found on the *Derfflinger*. The funnels do not have grilles moulded-in; photo-etch versions are included instead. The instructions follow the same format as for *Derfflinger*, with colour-coded sections showing where to place the deck fittings. The full colour painting and marking guide is also included.

The special edition version of the kit comes with eight brass barrels for the main armament and a torpedo boat. Despite the number of parts, modellers of limited experience will have no problems assembling either Flyhawk kit.

Below: Superstructure sprues showing the differences between *Derfflinger* (left) and *Lützow* (right)

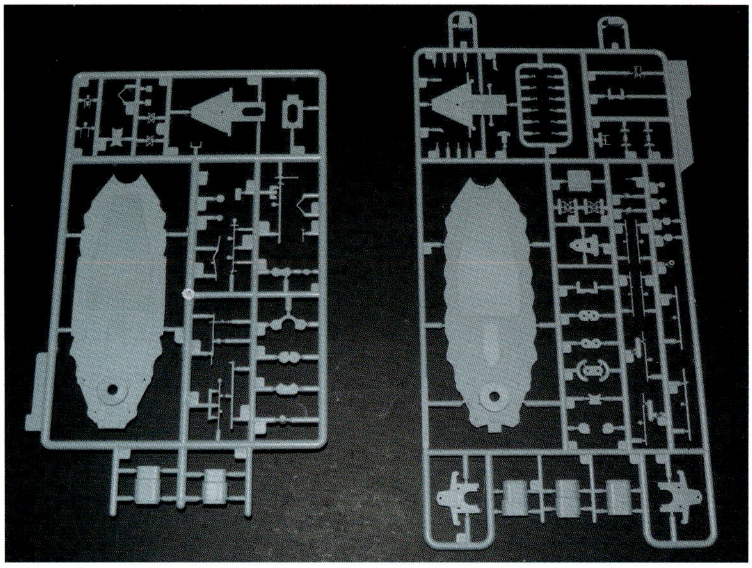

## HP ***HINDENBURG*** — 1:700 Scale

Right: Components of the HP *Hindenburg* kit

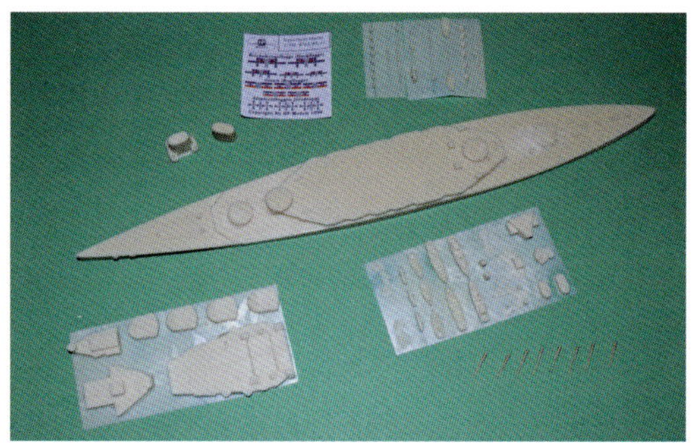

This kit of the last of the operational German battlecruisers features a one-piece resin cast hull completed up to the upper deck that scales out perfectly to 698 feet. The casting is very sharp, with well-defined casemates, breakwater, anchor chains, armour belt; the anchors are moulded on. The deck has a moderate level of detailing with finely scribed lines to represent the planking.

The rest of the main superstructure is crisply cast in three large pieces, with smaller parts such as boats, platforms, and searchlights on a separate resin wafer. The main gun turrets are the correct shape but lack any fine detail. The two-piece funnels feature the tall caps, but with inaccurate grilles. There are brass turned barrels for the main armament; the secondary casemate guns need their barrels to be created from plastic rod. There are three instruction sheets, one with an exploded view showing parts assembly, another with an overall drawing, and a parts list. A small sheet of flags is also included.

There are a few problems that the more experienced modeller may wish to correct. The breakwater is not correctly shaped (it should be curved rather than featuring sharp angles); nor is the superstructure completely accurate (drawings should be consulted to get this right); and the funnel caps on the real ship featured the standard lattice grilles, not the round holes found on the kit pieces. Despite these shortcomings, this kit will build up to a very nice-looking model right out of the box.

Right: Box art for the HP *Hindenburg*

## NNT ***MACKENSEN*** — 1:700 Scale

This kit splendidly captures the lines of this never-completed battlecruiser. The one-piece hull casting is complete up to the second superstructure deck, needing only the upper bridge work and funnels to be added. The quality of the casting is very good and it scales out accurately at 735 feet in length. The deck is very 'busy', with

plenty of smaller hatches, ventilators, scuttles, boat chocks and a very thin breakwater forward.

The main superstructure parts and the main gun turrets are on resin wafers, with boats and smaller details on separate resin casting plugs. The funnels have upper and lower pieces, with the upper having a moulded-in grille. The open boats are adequate, but the steam launches are not great representations of the real things, being a bit 'toy-like' in appearance. The main gun turrets are the correct shape and the resin gun barrels are adequate, but their appearance could be improved by drilling out the muzzles. Barrels for the casement guns are also supplied in resin, but barrels for the AA guns will have to be made from plastic rod. The lower masts are cast in resin, with the upper sections to be made from wire using the templates found in the instructions.

A photo-etch sheet with ladders, crane booms, davits, anchors, anchor chain and superstructure supports is included. There is also a masking sheet for the turret recognition markings and cord for the torpedo nets should the modeller wish to add them. There are two instruction sheets, one with an exploded view showing parts assembly, and the other a profile and plan drawing with painting instructions for the Humbrol range.

There are a lot of parts included with this kit; it will build into a very impressive model.

■ Review kits kindly lent by **Pavel Vacata** of **Admiralty Model Works** and **Leonard Fricke**

**Left:** Box art of the NNT *Mackensen*

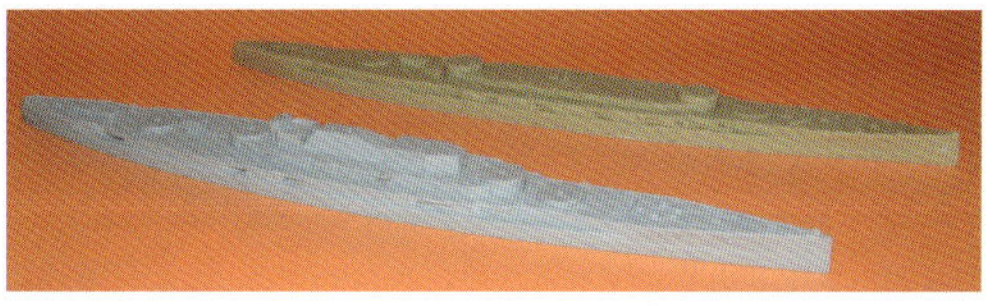

**Left:** *Mackensen* (rear) and *Ersatz Yorck* (front) hull castings

**Below:** Components of the NNT *Mackensen* kit

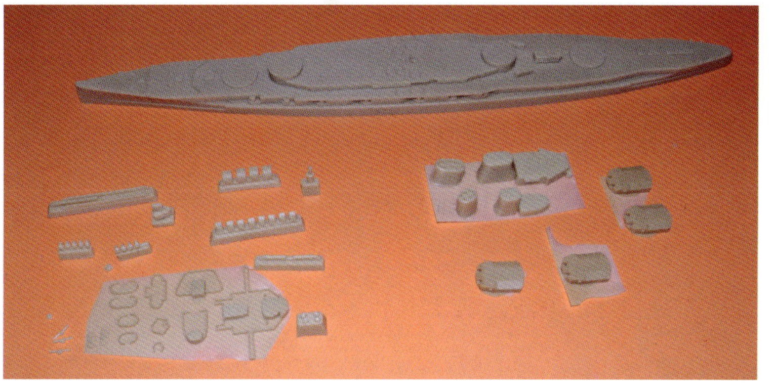

# IMPERIAL HOBBY PRODUCTIONS
# SMS 'ERSATZ YORCK' 1915 1:700 Scale

Imperial Hobby Productions produces a limited range of projected capital ships, including the British 'G3s', the US *Lexington* class battlecruisers, and this never-completed follow-on to the *Mackensen* class. The one-piece resin cast hull includes the entire main superstructure. As a consequence only the bridge and searchlight platforms need to be constructed in order to complete the basic model. The hull casting itself is very finely detailed and captures well the complex shapes of the hull and superstructure. The deck features individual planks with an adequate level of surface detail; ventilator intakes are also moulded in.

The main gun turrets are the correct shape, but are lacking in fine detail. Smaller parts such as boats, searchlights, anchors, and ventilators are cast on resin sprues. The single funnel amidships comes in two pieces with a high funnel cap featuring a moulded-in grille. The lattice work required for the searchlight platforms are cast as single resin blocks (probably best replaced with photo-etch from the spares box). The masts are supplied as pre-cut plastic rod, which is also supplied for the secondary armament gun barrels; the casemate fixing points for them will need to be drilled out. My kit example came with anchor chain and turned brass barrels for the main armament. There is a single page of instructions featuring a list of parts, profile and plan, and an exploded view showing parts assembly. There are no painting instructions.

This kit is no longer offered on Imperial Hobby Productions' web site, but it does appear from time to time at online auction sites. The 3D printing consortium known as Shapeways offers the main gun turrets and all the smaller parts for this kit as 3D printed parts. However, they do not provide the ship's boats.

■ Review kit kindly lent by **Leonard Fricke**

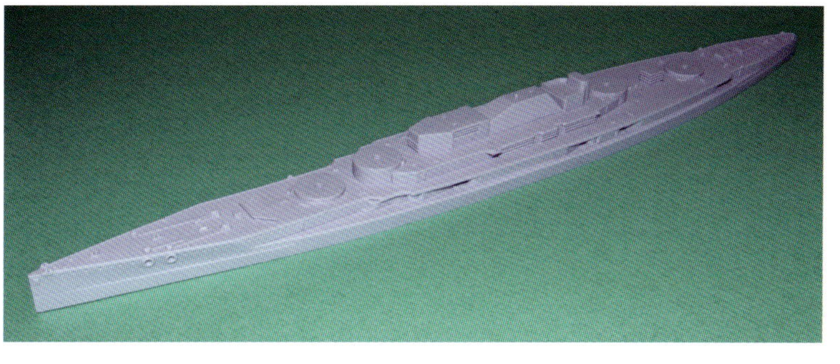

**Above:** Main hull casting clearly showing the air vents and complex shape of the hull

**Left:** Box art for the Imperial Hobbies *Ersatz Yorck*

# Photo-Etch & Accessories

In addition to the items reviewed in this section, standard accessories like railing, ladders, and cable reels are available from most companies that produce photo-etch details sets, such as Tom's Modelworks, Lion Roar, Gold Medal Models, and White Ensign.

## NNT BRASS GUN BARRELS 1:700 Scale

NNT supplies turned brass gun barrels for all the German battlecruiser and *Blücher* kits in 1:700 scale. They are all similar in style, with a hollowed muzzle and a spigot for attaching to the gun mount. The range consists of the main and secondary armament for all the ships: *Ersatz Yorck* 38cm (NNT B19), *Mackensen* 35cm (NNT B18), *Derfflinger* class 30.5cm (NNT B13), *Von der Tann*, *Moltke*, *Goeben*, and *Seydlitz* 28cm (NNT B01), *Blücher* 21cm (NNT B17) and the 15cm secondary armament carried aboard all of the ships (NNT B02).

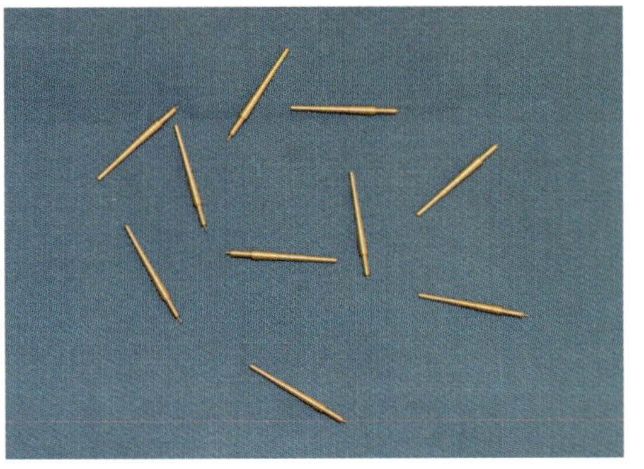

**Right:** 28cm gun barrels for *Von der Tann*, *Moltke*, *Goeben*, and *Seydlitz* *(Review photo courtesy NNT Models)*

## NNT 8.8CM GUN SHIELDS 1:700 Scale

These gun shields feature an open back providing an extra level of realism and detail compared with kit-supplied solid mouldings.

**Below:** NNT 8.8cm open back gun shields *(Review photo courtesy NNT Models)*

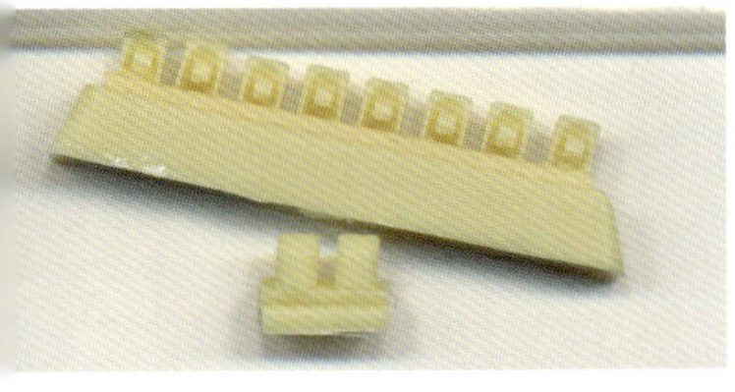

## NNT *MACKENSEN*, *GOEBEN*/*MOLTKE* PHOTO-ETCH SET 1:700 Scale

NNT supplies these photo-etch sheets with their *Mackensen* and *Goeben*/*Moltke* kits, but they can be ordered separately for use on other projects. Both sets are small, measuring approximately 2 x 1¼ inches, but contain very useful pieces – ladders, anchor chain, crane booms, davits, anchors, and superstructure supports. The set for *Mackensen* has oars for the open boats, and the *Goeben*/*Moltke* set also includes the heraldic bow shields and aerial spreaders for the masts.

**Above:** Etched brass sheet for *Goeben* and *Moltke* *(Review photo courtesy NNT Models)*

## FLYHAWK UPGRADE SETS *DERFFLINGER*/*LÜTZOW* 1:700 Scale

Not content with producing high quality plastic kits of the two German battlecruisers, Flyhawk also produces an upgrade set specific to each model. These are true multi-media sets with boxes crammed full of resin and turned brass parts and photo-etch sheets. There are literally hundreds of parts and, just as with the kits, the sets are not identical.

**Below:** Components of the Flyhawk *Derfflinger* upgrade set. **Inset:** Deck masking set from the *Lützow* upgrade set

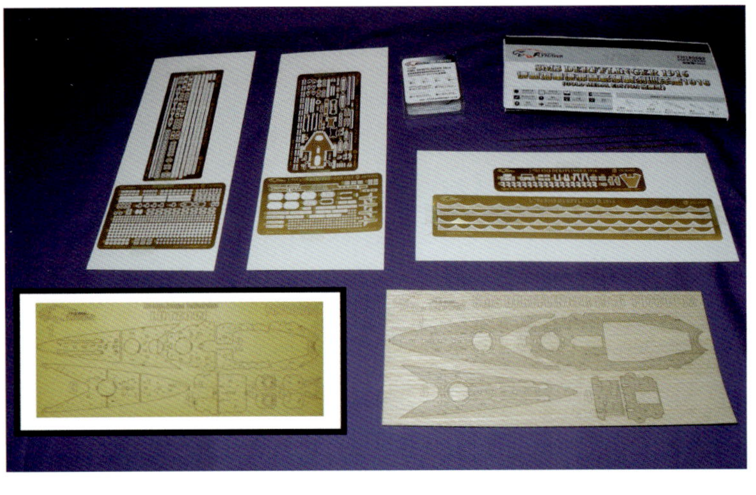

The set for *Derfflinger* has six photo-etch sheets which include railings already cut to the correct length for placing on the kit. There is a replacement bridge deck with railings already attached, bulkheads with relief-etched details and air vents, searchlight platform supports and storage lockers. It also features a laser-cut wood deck and brass rod for making the masts. There are no gun barrels for the main armament.

The set for *Lützow* has five photo-etch sheets. There are no railings as they are included in the basic kit, and there are no replacement decks or bulkheads. A deck masking set is supplied instead of a wooden deck. Masts and the main armament gun barrels are from turned brass. There are also funnels for the boats and foot ropes for the yardarms.

The following are the components common to both sets: resin pieces for the conning tower, aft control tower, shields for the 8.8cm guns, and lookout positions on the masts; secondary and 8.8cm gun barrels, torpedo net booms, capstans, bollards and crane posts from turned brass; cord for torpedo nets with photo-etch

**Left:** Box art for the Flyhawk *Lützow* upgrade set

securing hoops; photo-etch anchors, doors, boat chocks, covers for the portholes, searchlight covers, davits, funnel handrails, funnel grilles, cabins, oars, rudders, and thwarts for the boats, hose reels, crane booms and hooks, coaling port hatches, and searchlight platforms. Most intriguing are the deployed torpedo nets that are found in both sets, done in photo-etch with turned brass torpedo net booms. The instructions are very extensive, with colour coding showing how to fold and place each part including the railings and torpedo nets.

These are very high quality sets, with the precision and detail of the turned brass components particularly exquisite. These upgrade sets provide plenty of scope for super-detailing Flyhawk kits that are already very good right from the box.

■ Review sets courtesy of **Flyhawk Model**

## BMK *SEYDLITZ* MAST SET 1:350 Scale

BMK produces a complete set of turned brass masts for the Combrig *Seydlitz* kit, comprising two-piece mainmast, a two-piece foremast, and separate yards and mastheads. The set is now out of production, but in future may be available from SSN Modellbau, who took over the corresponding BMK gun barrel set for *Seydlitz*.

■ Review samples courtesy **Roger Torgeson**

**Below:** Masts From left to right: two-piece mainmast, two-piece foremast, yards, and mastheads

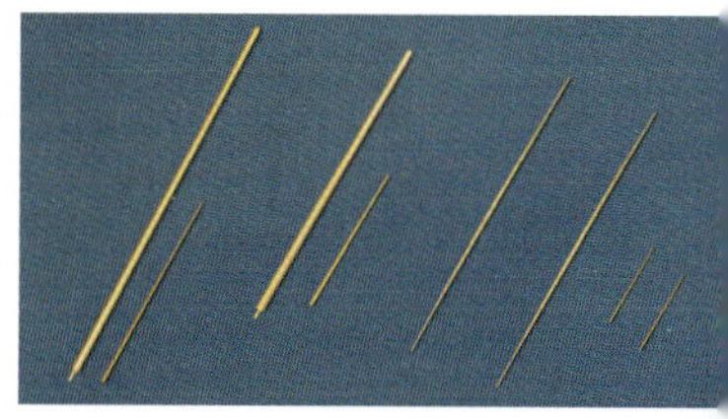

## BMK *SEYDLITZ* BRASS GUN BARRELS 1:350 Scale

BMK makes a complete set of gun barrels in brass for the Combrig *Seydlitz* kit, comprising the 28cm main armament, 15cm secondaries, and the 8.8cm AA/anti-torpedo-boat guns – 34 gun barrels in total, all with hollowed-out muzzles. BMK has turned production of these items over to SSN Modellbau who lists them as item BM-350-002.

■ Review samples courtesy **Roger Torgeson**

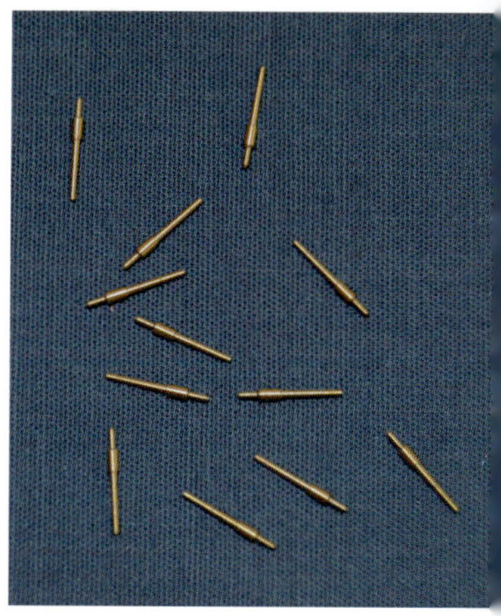

**Above:** BMK 8.8cm brass barrels

## ARTWOX, WOOD HUNTER *VON DER TANN/DERFFLINGER* 1:700 Scale

At time of writing (2015), there are two commercially available wooden decks for German battlecruisers, both in 1:700 scale. Artwox produces a deck for the Combrig *Von der Tann* 1910 (Item AW20089); Wood Hunter has a deck for the Flyhawk *Derfflinger* (Item W70046). Both decks come with anchor chain. Wood Hunter also provides a photo-etch sheet of coaling ports and boat chocks.

The Artwox deck for *Von der Tann* has a large piece for the main deck, with three smaller pieces for the forecastle and the tops of the embrasures on the stern quarters. The Wood Hunter deck for *Derfflinger* is in four pieces: forecastle, quarterdeck, amidships superstructure deck, and the upper boat deck. The instructions for both sets are very simple, with drawings or photos showing how the deck should appear when glued in place, what needs to be removed prior to installation, and where to place the photo-etch replacement pieces once the deck is glued in place.

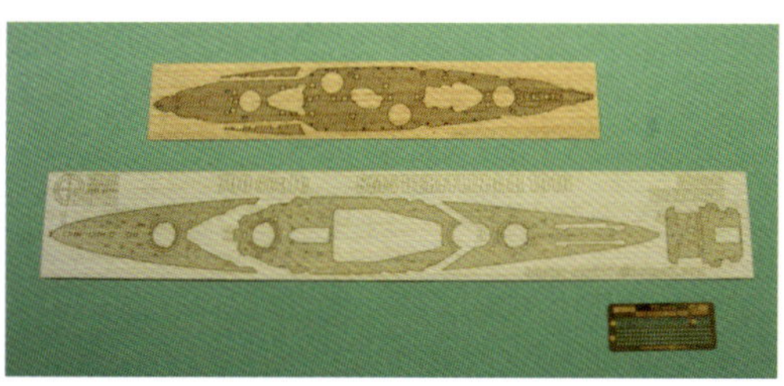

**Left:** At top is the Artwox deck for the Combrig *Von der Tann*. Below is the Wood Hunter deck and photo-etch sheet for the Flyhawk *Derfflinger*

The decks are similar in construction, consisting of an incredibly thin laser-cut wood deck with finely detailed deck planking, backed with a layer of peel and stick self-adhesive. There are cut-outs to fit over deck hatches and other deck detail; these need to be punched out with a sharp knife. Careful layout over the kit deck will be required, paying close attention to which deck details need to project through the wood deck. These wooden decks radically change a model's appearance and will elicit a lot of favourable comment at hobby shows.

## VTH SHIP PLANS 1:125 Scale

For those interested in scratch building or in super detailing one of the battlecruiser kits, VTH carries large scale sets of deck plans for *Seydlitz* (Item 3204005, 5 sheets), *Lützow* (Item 3204006, 5 sheets) and *Goeben* (Item 3204007, 4 sheets).

# Modelmakers' Showcase

## HMV *VON DER TANN* 1:250 scale

By HORST LUECKE

This model depicts *Von der Tann* as commissioned in 1910 and is built from the HMV paper model kit. The railings and anchor chains came from the photo-etch set produced by HMV specifically for this kit.

The build was fairly straightforward using the kit instructions. The edges of any folded parts need to be painted so that they don't stand out on the finished model, much like using putty on plastic or resin kits.

The basic tools used were a scalpel, steel ruler, a good pair of tweezers and some needles and wood dowels to help form the small parts.

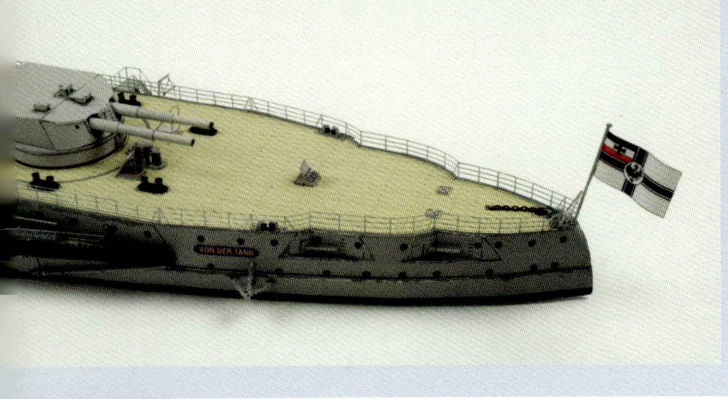

(Photos by Benjamin Fentens - HMV)

## COMBRIG *LÜTZOW* 1:700 scale

By KOSTAS KATSEAS

**Kostas Katseas** writes:
As is usual with Combrig kits the casting was flawless, no warping and no flash. The detail is sharp, especially on the deck, and the dimensions of the kit and the lines of the hull are spot on. My only criticism would be the lack of detail on the superstructure bulkheads. The model benefited from extra photo-etch portholes, doors, fire hoses, etc. The first, and probably trickiest, part of the build was the construction of the masts from brass rod. After that the assembly was rather simple and quick.

This was a commissioned build with a request for some extra weathering in the form of some visible patina on the hull sides. The sea was left moderate to calm, enhancing the elegant lines of this ship. It is a kit I would recommend for the beginner to the advanced builder as it provides an excellent base for a model of the *Lützow*.

# NNT *GOEBEN* 1:700 scale

By NORBERT THIEL

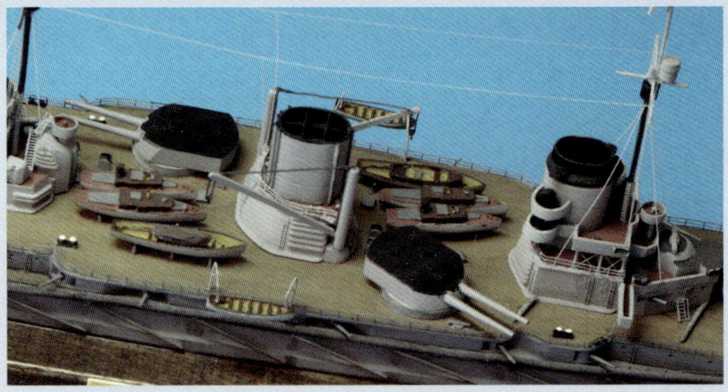

**Norbert Thiel** writes:
*Goeben* is shown here under the Turkish flag, retaining her torpedo nets but minus two 15cm secondary guns that were removed for defence of the Dardanelles. The kit-supplied photo-etch sheet was used for many of the small details; railings are from Tom's Modelworks and rigging from stretched sprue. Metal gun barrels for the 20cm and 15cm mounts are from NNT. The hull was painted in Tamiya XF-54 + 40% XF-19, the superstructure with Tamiya XF-19 + 20% XF-2. The Turkish flag was gnerated on a computer.

# WSW *DERFLINGER* 1:700 scale

By JIM BAUMANN

**Jim Baumann** writes:
This model was built back in 1997 when this resin kit was considered 'state of the art'. It was extensively modified and refined in those pre-Internet days using the best available printed resource to hand (*Die Grossen Kreuzer* by Koop and Schmolke). The boat cranes and the large distinctive midships boat davits were made using offcuts of photo-etch that were glued and soldered together. The clunky cast funnel handrails were pared off and replaced using fine copper wire. The funnels were drilled out as well. The wheelhouse was remade along with an all-metal bridge-deck cut out

of brass sheet. The masts were made from stainless steel.

Despite being an old model I feel it still holds up quite well to builds of the ship using a modern kit. Having spent all its time away from UV sunlight in a glass display case, none of the resin parts show any sign of warping and all stretched sprue rigging is still fully intact.

# IRON SHIPWRIGHTS *SEYDLITZ* 1:350 scale

By TONY VAN WYK

**Tony van Wyk** writes:

I had actually completed this model when I obtained several references including *Warship Profile 14: SMS Seydlitz* and *Die Grossen Kreuzer*. After careful study, I realized there were a number of major errors in the ISW kit. The two biggest are a missing casemate position aft of the portside No 2 casemate and the addition of a casement directly under the portside wing turret; also, the centre superstructure with the aft funnel and the starboard wing turret are slightly too far forward.

I had to dismantle the entire ship, removing the centre and rear superstructures, the main armament barbettes, and skylights, and sanding the deck smooth. The torpedo net shelves were also removed as I wanted to depict the ship in her post-Jutland fit. Having drilled out the new portside casemate and filled in the incorrect one under the port wing turret, I replaced the kit-supplied 15cm and 8.8cm casemate guns with those from an ICM *König* kit, which required some work to make room for the new guns.

After this was complete I added a new deck of Evergreen grooved plastic sheet, drilling out bow and stern anchor hawse pipes. The aft superstructure was reconstructed using the *König*'s conning tower with new louvered structures added to each side and in front of the conning tower. The searchlight platforms were replaced with thin plastic card, the searchlights and 8.8cm guns being replaced with those from the *König* kit. Many of the existing louvers were replaced or enhanced using thin plastic card after drilling out the area behind them in order to provide a bit of depth.

I made and installed new crane masts and derricks to the centre superstructure, hollowed out the funnel, and used plastic rod to add piping on the exterior of the funnel. The centre superstructure and the starboard wing turret were then positioned slightly further aft than where the kit had them located. I replaced all the decks and platforms on the forward superstructure with thin plastic card, brass rod being used to add the supports for the various decks and platforms. The forward conning tower and the searchlights were replaced with the ones from the *König* kit.

The main turrets from the *König* kit were modified by carefully removing the sides and back, then reducing the turrets to the correct dimensions for the *Seydlitz* before reattaching the sides and rear, thus retaining almost all of the surface rivet detail. The barrels were also shortened to the correct length for the *Seydlitz*'s 28cm guns. Bollards, ships boats, capstans, anchors and various deck fittings also came from the *König* kit.

The White Ensign photo-etch sheet for *König* was used throughout as necessary for railings, hatches, and the deadlights for the forward and aft superstructure scuttles. The last things to be added were the fore and aft masts in the post-Jutland configuration. White Ensign Colourcoats were used for painting.

## WSW *DERFFLINGER* 1:700 scale

By NORBERT THIEL

**Norbert Thiel** writes:
Another fine kit from WSW built mostly from the box using NNT photo-etch for some details; railings are from Tom's Modelworks. The crane booms were left as supplied and not corrected. Torpedo net booms and mast detail were done in copper wire with rigging from stretched sprue. The kit-supplied 30cm and 15cm gun barrels were replaced with NNT brass barrels. The hull was painted using Tamiya XF-54 + 40% XF-19, the superstructure in XF-19 + 20% XF-2, with the after funnel in red as it would have appeared as the ship went into action at Jutland.

# WSW *LÜTZOW* 1:700 scale

By NICK DOGGER

**Nick Dogger** writes:
Modifications to the basic kit included opening hatches and companionways and hollowing out the funnels. Canvas dodgers were added around the superstructure and bridge railings, along with eyebrows and covers to the scuttles. The torpedo nets were from cord with thin wire bindings and the rigging and funnel grilles were made from stretched plastic sprue. The photo-etch railings and the brass gun barrels were supplied separately. Some weathering was added when painting the model to try to depict the effect of salt spray and coal smoke on the ship in actual service.

# SCRATCH-BUILT *LÜTZOW* 1:350 scale

By TONY VAN WYK

**Tony van Wyk** writes:
This was my first scratch-build of an entire ship, took about a year to complete, and used an excellent set of plans produced by Verlag fur Technik und Handwerk (VTH). The three sheets detailing the ship were in 1:125 and two others of ship's equipment were in varying scales from 1:5 to 1:50. I reduced the originals to a constant set of paper plans at 1:350 and then cut out the various shapes for use as templates, which were then glued to styrene plastic sheets and cut out. This technique worked quite well for the entire ship, but I would recommend using a good set of drafting tools. The main deck was made from Evergreen grooved plastic sheet, using the narrowest grooved sheet that they make.

The main, secondary, and 8.8cm armament came from an ICM *König* kit, along with the ship's boats, the forward and aft conning towers, searchlights, deck fittings, cranes and any other parts that I found uses for. The White Ensign photo-etch sheet for *König* was also used almost in its entirety including the torpedo net shelves, supports, and davits; the torpedo nets themselves are from shoelaces. White Ensign Colourcoats were used for painting. The base was my first attempt at a seascape and is an acrylic gel that has been stippled with a paintbrush then painted with gloss blue.

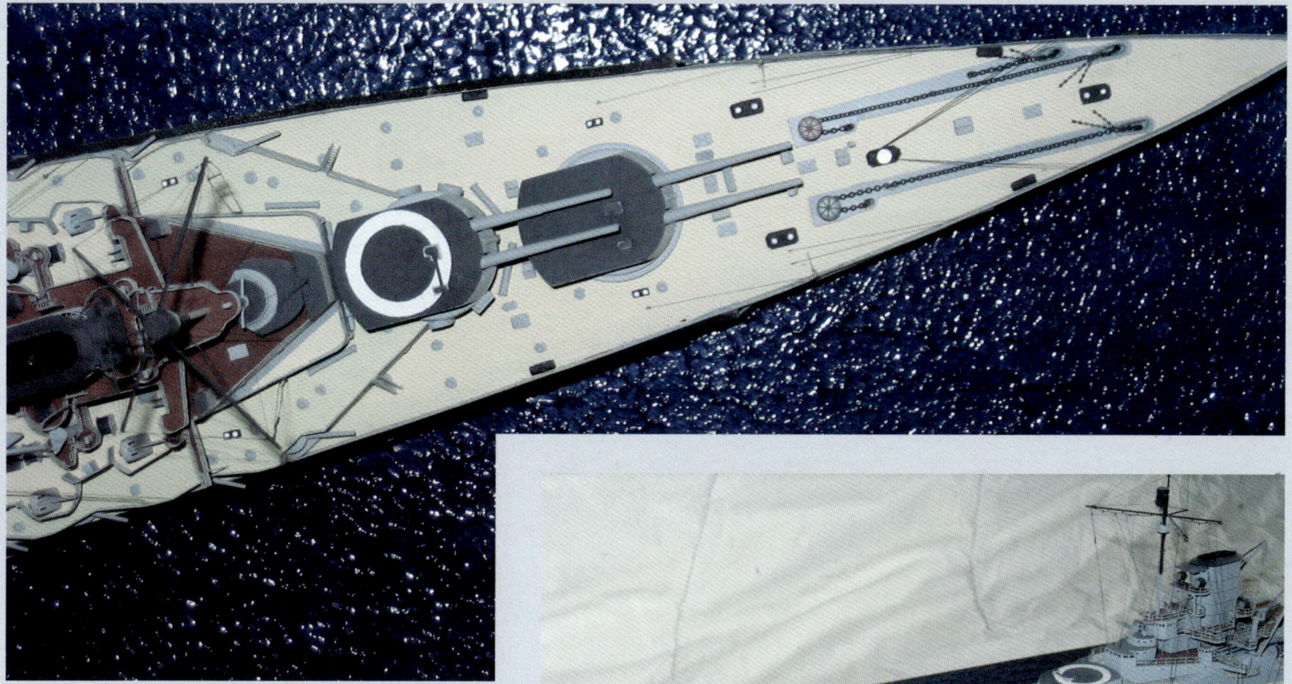

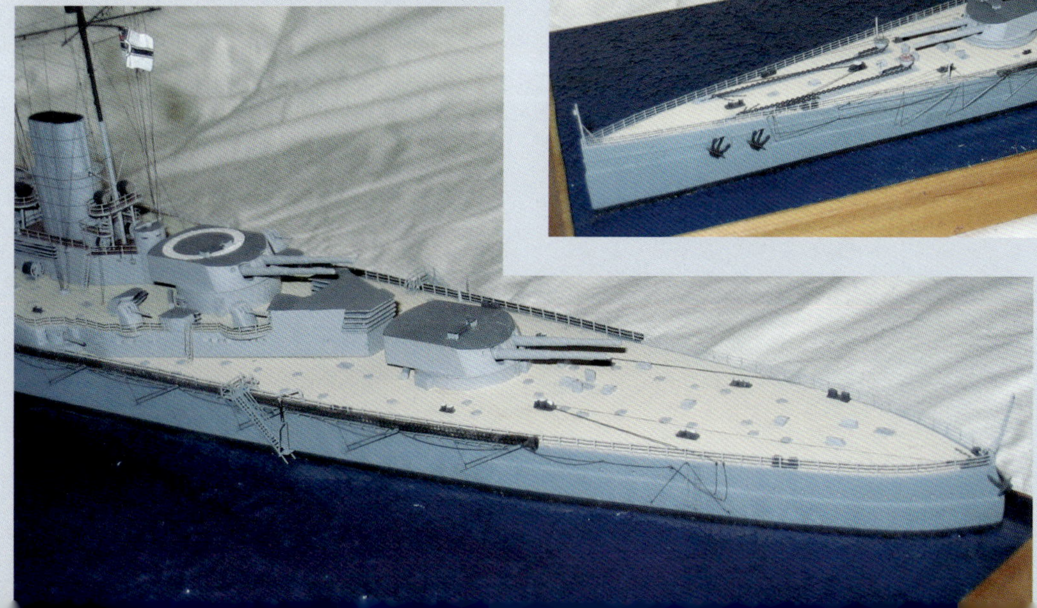

# NNT *MACKENSEN* 1:700 scale

By KOSTAS KATSEAS

**Kostas Katseas** writes:
This kit comes with a basic count of bits covering the main turrets, superstructure and funnel parts, and the masts. Smaller details on the bulkheads of the superstructures are rather limited to a few portholes and raised doors, which would greatly benefit from the addition of some photo-etch replacements and additional fittings. The casting was very clean with very nice engraved deck planking lines, and my copy showed almost no warping, a common problem with resin kits. The kit builds to an impressive model, and as the vessel is large one can add extra levels of detail such as a more complicated bridge structure with additional platforms. Since the ship was never completed, historical accuracy is not a concern, at least not for the upperworks.

The model was depicted making a hard turn, probably during sea trials, requiring a small portion of plastic sheet to be added to depict part of the lower hull. This was easy as the ship had no bulges or additional curves on the hull.

# NNT *MOLTKE* 1:700 scale

By NICK DOGGER

**Nick Dogger** writes:
To provide greater accuracy and interest, the basic kit was modified with extra details. Hatches and companionways were opened, the funnels hollowed out, and the main armour belt was thinned for better scale effect. The vent louvres on the kit were replaced with ones made with individual slats. Canvas dodgers were added to the superstructure railings, and the scuttles were detailed with eyebrows and covers. Cord with thin wire bindings was employed for the torpedo nets, and the rigging and funnel grilles were made from stretched plastic sprue. Separately supplied photo-etch railings and brass gun barrels were used. In an effort to show the effects of salt spray and coal smoke, appropriate weathering was applied when painting the model.

## HMV *DERFFLINGER* 1:250 scale By HORST LUECKE

This model depicts *Derfflinger* as she appeared after Jutland with the tripod foremast and was built straight from the HMV paper model kit. The railings and anchor chains came from the photo-etch set produced by HMV specifically for this kit. Even though the kit comes completely pre-coloured, it is necessary to paint the edges of the paper parts to get the result shown in the accompanying pictures. Rigging was done using the diagrams provided in the kit instructions.

*(Photos by Benjamin Fentens - HMV)*

# HP *HINDENBURG* 1:700 scale

By JIM BAUMANN

**Jim Baumann** writes:
This model depicts the *Hindenburg* after being scuttled in Scapa Flow. The time frame is 1920, with the ship seen at low tide with the bow just breaking the surface. She is sitting on the bottom, with some of the more portable items having been removed. This project was very complex due to the nature of the diorama and because this very early HP kit of the ship was really rather inaccurate in most areas. Fortunately most of the ship was to be submerged and I had photos and some excerpts from the original plans for reference. The entire forward superstructure and the upper masts were completely scratch-built and the funnels with their surrounding structures were heavily modified.

The priority of this project was to simulate the water in such a manner that when viewed from directly overhead the viewer can 'just' make out the outline of the hull; whilst when viewed from a non-elevated position the water appears to be opaque. (Scapa Flow is very tidal and there is much water-borne silt making the water appear cloudy.) The water was made using Artists' medium Acrylic Gel, which the enclosed

instructions clearly direct to apply in thin layers. However I elected instead to apply the total thickness of 25mm in one go. It took 14 months in a heated linen cupboard surrounded by bags of silica gel to eventually dry clear. On top of the gel went numerous additional layers of white glue and varnish to eventually bring the water level to the desired height. Often the layers were coloured with very thin washes of watercolour paint to give translucence and opacity. Plenty of scope for 'over weathering'!

# SCRATCH-BUILT *SEYDLITZ* 1:1200 scale

By JEFFREY STEVENSON

This model was inspired by a well-known photo, shown below, taken of *Seydlitz* as she made her last journey to the breaker's yard in 1930. The hull and all its fittings are all hand-crafted in white metal. Creating the hull was a two-part process. A basic hull was made from modelling clay, a silicon rubber mould was made, and a white metal hull was cast. This first basic white metal hull was then shaped to accurately reflect the complex shape of *Seydlitz*'s underwater hull, and docking strakes and bilge keels were added. Another silicon rubber mould was then created and the finished hull was cast from it.

Masters for the rudder, propeller, huts, and airlocks were created from plastic card and then cast in white metal using moulds made from the masters. Once the fittings were placed, the model was painted to reflect what *Seydlitz* would have looked like after nine years on the bottom of Scapa Flow. The tugs are a generic design based on a typical harbour tug of the 1920s and were also cast in white metal from a master created using plastic card.

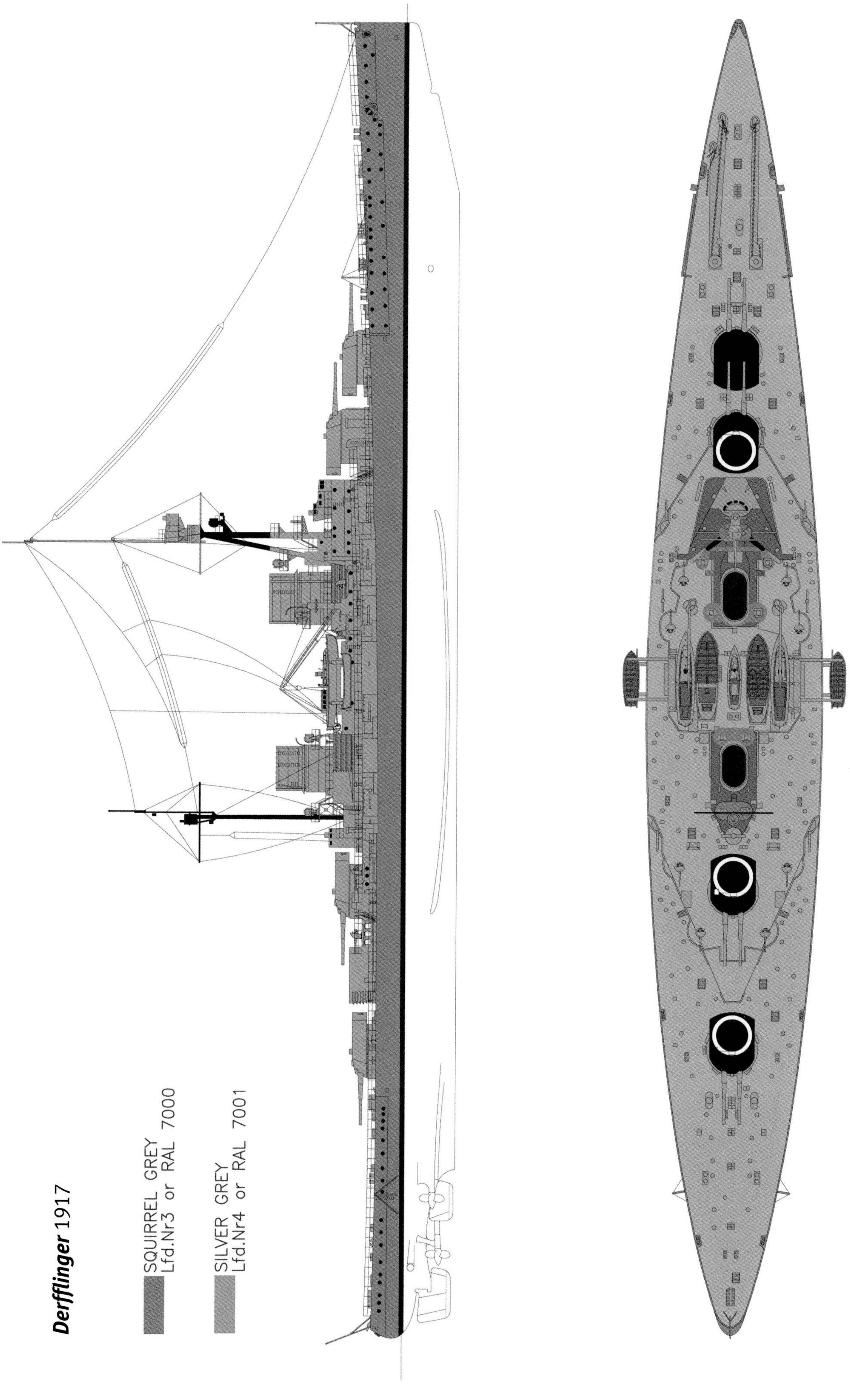
Derfflinger 1917
SQUIRREL GREY
Lfd.Nr3 or RAL 7000
SILVER GREY
Lfd.Nr4 or RAL 7001

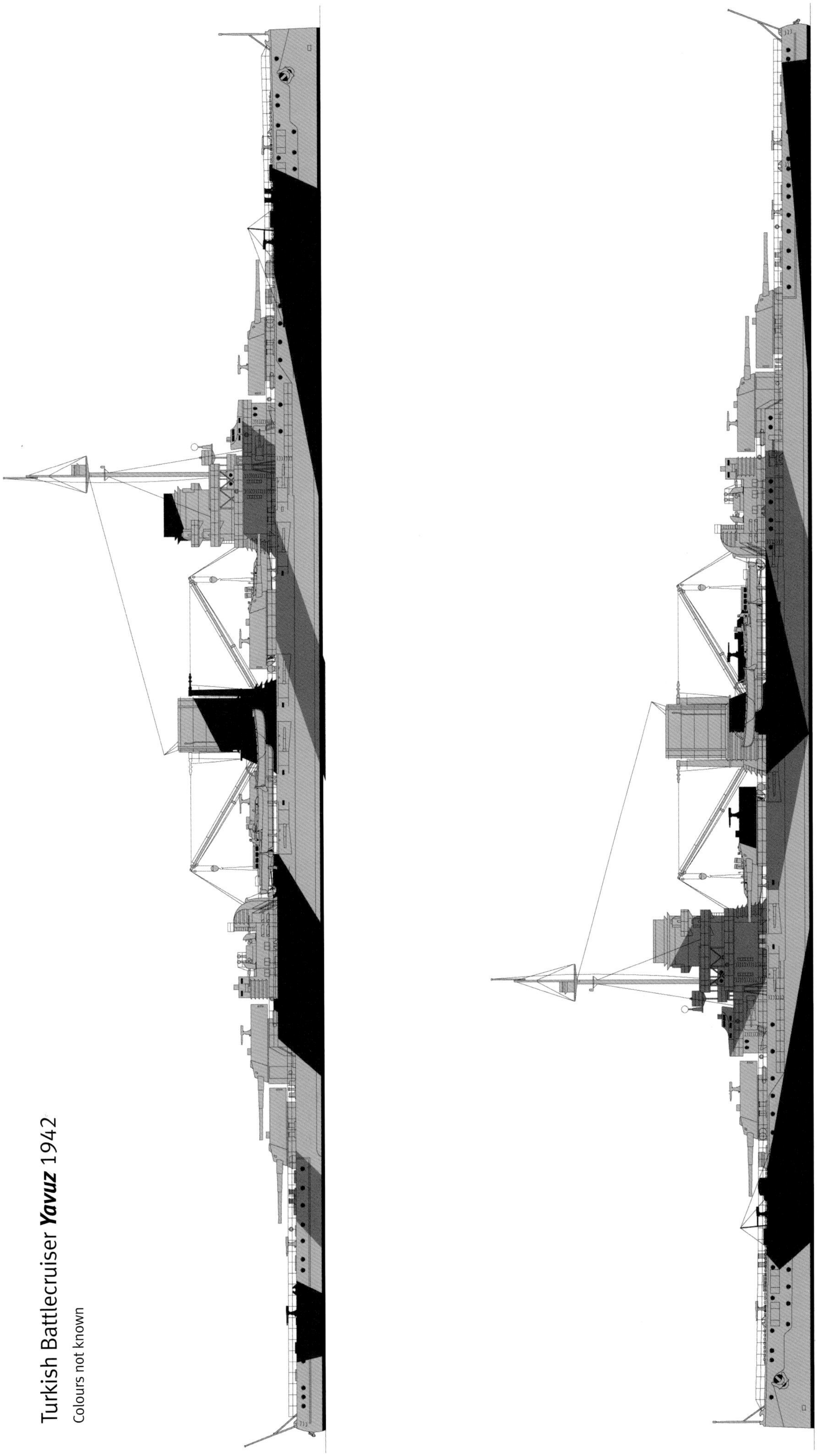

Turkish Battlecruiser ***Yavuz*** 1942

Colours not known

# Appearance

Because of their short lifespan and wartime conditions, there were no radical appearance changes made to the German battlecruisers. Even after the very long life of the *Goeben*, in 1970 she could still be recognised as the same ship which was first commissioned into the Kaiser's fleet in 1911. One change made by all of the ships was the removal of the torpedo net defence system (excluding *Hindenburg*, to which it was never fitted). This consisted of a steel mesh net stowed rolled up on a net shelf that extended beyond the hull sides, almost the length of the ship, and a series of booms hinged along the lower hull. This system had been used by a number of navies for many years. In theory, when the ship was at anchor or travelling at very low speed, with the booms swung out the net would be deployed far enough outboard of the hull to stop or explode torpedoes aimed at the ship before they could strike the hull. The Royal Navy also used the same system but discovered in 1915 that the system was totally ineffective. On 27 May, when the old pre-dreadnought battleship HMS *Majestic* was at anchor with the anti-torpedo nets fully deployed, a torpedo from *U 27* went through the net and struck the hull, sinking the ship. Realising the net system was totally useless topweight, most of the capital ships of the Royal Navy landed their nets and booms before the Battle of Jutland. At this battle all of the German battlecruisers were still carrying theirs, and during the fighting it became clear that instead of the system offering protection in limited circumstances, their presence was a hazard in combat operations. As the ships received battle damage the nets came loose and would drag in the water, reducing speed because of the increased resistance. In the case of *Von der Tann*, the nets did not threaten to foul the propellers and therefore could be cut away while moving, but *Derfflinger*'s damaged nets trailed above the port propeller, so the ship had to come to a total stop to cut away the nets to eliminate the danger to the propeller. Fortunately for the battlecruiser she was not under observation or fire at the time, which was in late afternoon in poor visibility during the escape from the Grand Fleet. As part of the repairs following the battle, all of the German battlecruisers had their nets and booms removed.

**Above:** As completed *Blücher* carried light pole masts and in general silhouette was not unlike the *Von der Tann* which followed her. She is seen here in 1912. *(Bundesarchiv 26-61-11)*

## BLÜCHER

*Blücher* was completed with a light pole foremast, but in 1913 she became the first German warship to be fitted with a tripod, as used by the Royal Navy, when the pole foremast was replaced with a tripod mast and larger control top.

## VON DER TANN

This ship received only minimal alterations. As the threat from the Royal Navy aircraft increased during the war, it was realised

**Left:** *Blücher* in 1914 after the fitting of the first tripod mast in the German navy; yardarms forming an X shape in plan view were shipped at the same time and the ensemble looks like a prototype for the arrangement later adopted in *Hindenburg* and *Derfflinger*.

Detail views of *Von der Tann* at the Coronation Fleet Review at Spithead in June 1911. *(©National Maritime Museum G05472 & N11086)*

**Left:** This amidships view of *Von der Tann* shows many details of fittings, even though the focus of the photo is the bread delivery in the foreground.

**Left:** An aerial shot of *Von der Tann* at the end of the war. The main points of interest are wartime modifications: spotting tops on both masts, a reconstructed aft superstructure with two 8.8cm Flak L/45 AA guns added, and the original hull casemates for 8.8cm SK guns plated over. The ship also has white circle aerial recognition markings on 'A' and 'D' main turrets, although the paintwork has faded. *(©National Maritime Museum L5844)*

that anti-aircraft artillery needed to be added. The ship had completed with four 8.8cm SK surface guns, which were designed as anti-torpedo-boat defence. In 1916 the low-angle 8.8cm guns were removed from the aft superstructure and two 8.8cm Flak L/45 guns were fitted for anti-aircraft defence. Also in 1916, spotting tops were added to both masts and the compass cage/structure was removed from the aft superstructure. Other casemate-mounted 8.8cm SK guns at the bow and stern were removed and their positions plated over, as they were of dubious benefit given their light weight of shell and the low freeboard of the battlecruiser, which only allowed their use in calm weather.

## *MOLTKE*

As completed, *Moltke* had low, flat funnel caps, but shortly after completion a prominent raised cap/cowling was added to the fore funnel. At the end of 1912 the forward superstructure was modified and the upper searchlight platform extended forward to include a new admiral's bridge to fit the ship for her role as flagship. A small spotting top was added to the foremast in 1914. Other changes to the *Moltke* were similar to those received by *Von der Tann*. The aft superstructure 8.8cm SK surface-fire guns

**Below:** *Moltke* as first modified with a cap on the fore funnel, but before the bridge was extended at the end of 1912. *(©National Maritime Museum A2539)*

**Top and above:** Once the program of trials had been completed, *Moltke* was sent on a high-level goodwill mission to the USA, which included a presidential visit to the ship. The ship then visited New York from 9 to 13 July, as seen in these two views – the ship had been repainted after the Atlantic crossing, and in strong sunshine looks immaculate.

**Above, right:** This close-up of *Goeben*'s forward hull and superstructure from sea level shows a host of small fitting detail, including the complex run of the rigging to the anti-torpedo nets. One of the four-part hinged covers to the forward 8.8cm mountings is open. The ship is pretty much as completed. *(Bundesarchiv 134-C0047)*

**Below:** *Moltke* after the Armistice, interned at Scapa. The original glass-plate negative is broken, but otherwise it is a very clear portrait of the ship in her final guise.

**Above:** The Turkish *Yavuz* (ex-*Goeben*) visiting Malta in 1936. Following a repair and refit carried out by a French company in 1927–30, the ship was recommissioned with a modified bridge structure and some additional machine guns. The ship was later given a more radical modernisation in 1941.

**Left:** *Yavuz* (ex-*Goeben*) at Istanbul in May 1947, still wearing the remains of the three-tone camouflage adopted during the Second World War. The effects of the major modernisation in 1941 can be seen in the absence of the old mainmast and the large number of single AA guns on turret roofs and around the after superstructure.

were replaced by four 8.8cm Flak L/45 AA guns (actually, dual-purpose on C/1913 mountings) in 1916 and the hull-mounted 8.8cm SK guns were removed and the casemates plated over.

## GOEBEN

On completion the *Goeben* was very similar in appearance to her sister ship. However, they could be distinguished from one another in certain aspects. Unlike *Moltke*, *Goeben* was completed with a prominent forward funnel cap/cowling but it was shorter than the one fitted to the *Moltke* in 1912. The aft funnel of *Goeben* was not jacketed, as in *Moltke*, so it was very slightly thinner and was flat across the top, lacking the low, flat cap of *Moltke*. A small spotting top was added to the foremast in 1914, although it is not clear where the work was carried out – possibly at Constantinople after the ship's arrival there in August. In May 1915 the fourth 5.9in secondary gun on each side was landed to provide additional coastal defence guns for the Dardanelles. *Goeben* also received four 8.8cm Flak guns, replacing the surface-fire 8.8cm SK guns on the aft superstructure in 1916. After modernisation and repairs were completed in 1930, four machine guns were added to the forward superstructure.

The greatest appearance change for the *Goeben*, or for any of the German battlecruisers, came in 1941 during a major refit designed to provide modern anti-aircraft protection. The aft mast was removed to improve arcs of fire and the ship received a huge increase in her AA gun complement. She acquired an additional four single 8.8cm AA guns on the after superstructure, eight single gun 40mm guns (four on the

**Above:** *Seydlitz* in 1913, as completed.

**Right:** Looking aft along the starboard side of *Seydlitz* during a wartime practice shoot. Note the bands on the after funnel; these were painted white pre-war, but although they were later painted over in grey, the raised metal band remained. From about 1917 a number of standard-pattern large square life rafts were added to many German warships; one can be seen on the side of the wing turret. *(Bundesarchiv 134-B4239)*

**Right:** *Seydlitz* during the first half of the war – she carries the small spotting top fitted in 1914 but is still fitted with the anti-torpedo nets that were removed after Jutland.

**Left:** *Derfflinger* as completed, with a small spotting top on the foremast and four 8.8cm SK guns in casemates in the forward superstructure (removed in 1915). The gap between the third and fourth 5.9in casemates was filled by an extra gun in *Lützow*.

forecastle and two on each of the amidships turret crowns) and four single 20mm guns, with one centreline at the bow, two at the stern and one on the crown of 'D' turret.

## SEYDLITZ

A spotting top was added to the foremast in 1914. The two aft superstructure 8.8cm surface action guns were replaced by two 8.8cm AA guns before Jutland in 1916. In common with the other battlecruisers, the casemate 8.8cm SK guns were removed and their positions over-plated.

## DERFFLINGER AND *LÜTZOW*

The three ships of the *Derfflinger* class were easily distinguished by their funnels. *Derfflinger* completed with high funnel caps/cowlings above the funnel jacket and a fore funnel slightly higher than the aft funnel. *Lützow* was completed with funnels of equal height and the jacket of the fore funnel was extended all the way to the top during final fitting out. *Hindenburg* had funnels of equal height with prominent caps/cowlings above the jacket but the cowlings were shorter than those fitted on *Derfflinger*. *Lützow*, fitted as a flagship, was completed with an extra level added to the bridge, and also carried an additional pair of 5.9in guns. In *Derfflinger* the four forward 8.8cm surface-fire SK guns under the bridge were removed and the casemates plated over in 1915; they were replaced with four 8.8cm Flak L/45 AA guns clustered around the forward funnel. The four after 88m SK mounts were landed after Jutland, but they do not seem to have been replaced by AA mounts. The two forward 8.8cm AA guns were removed before the surrender. *Lützow* was completed without any 8.8cm guns, but two AA mounts were added abreast 'C' turret in April 1916, and two more the following month; the positions for four more either side of the fore funnel were never filled. Both ships had pole foremasts at Jutland, but after the battle *Derfflinger* received a heavy tripod foremast during her repairs.

## HINDENBURG

The *Hindenburg* was slightly longer than the other two and during completion the

**Below:** An aerial view of *Derfflinger* as modified after Jutland. The principal alteration was the fitting of a massive tripod foremast, with legs more widely splayed than *Hindenberg*'s. The four after 8.8cm AA guns around 'C' turret have been removed, but the two either side of the fore funnel are still in place in this photo, although the forward pair were landed before the end of the war. The ship has white aerial recognition circles painted on all four main turrets, although that on 'A' is very faded. Like many other German warships of this period, the ship has had a number of life rafts added. *(Bundesarchiv 134-B0115)*

**Right:** A quarter view of *Lützow* at Kiel, hoisting out one of the ship's motor boats. From this angle it is easy to see the difference between the funnels, and how they varied from those of *Derfflinger* and *Hindenberg*. The 8.8cm AA mounts around 'C' turret do not seem to be fitted yet. *(Bundesarchiv 134-C1452)*

**Far right:** The forward superstructure and bridge of *Hindenberg* differed from her two near-sisters, notably in the tripod mast and the enclosed compass platform above the admiral's bridge. In this undated view, the forward 8.8cm AA mounting abreast the funnel is missing – the ship ran trials without any of them – but she was carrying all four when interned at Scapa. *(Bundesarchiv 134-D0024)*

same heavy tripod foremast fitted to *Derfflinger* was also fitted to *Hindenburg*, although the legs were less splayed. She never had any provision for 8.8cm guns in the surface-fire SK version, but carried two Flak L/45 AA mountings either side of the fore funnel. *Hindenburg* was the only German battlecruiser never to carry the torpedo net and boom system, but was fitted to handle two floatplanes, one either side of the aft funnel, lowered into the water and recovered by a light derrick.

## CAMOUFLAGE AND PAINT SCHEMES

Unlike the Royal Navy, which adopted true camouflage schemes near the end of the war, primarily to confuse U-boat commanders, the Imperial German Navy never designed a specific camouflage pattern. However, the normal German paint scheme functioned very well to hide the ships in the mists normally encountered in the North Sea. The hull was painted a slightly darker grey than the superstructure but both tones could be called light grey. This same paint scheme was carried forward to the German warships built for the Third Reich until they did adopt specific camouflage designs. However, the Kaiser's navy was a ground-breaker when it came to aerial recognition markings. At the start of the war and definitely until at least 1917, the German Navy held a significant advantage in the field of naval aerial reconnaissance, in the form of the extensive and capable Zeppelin fleet. German naval operations almost always incorporated Zeppelin reconnaissance, although typical weather conditions in the North Sea usually negated the effort. The Royal Navy had nothing comparable, as their dirigible program was an abysmal flop. It is interesting to note that the threat of Zeppelins and the failure of British efforts to use the same technology, drove the Royal Navy to develop the aircraft carrier. Major German warships had dark grey turret tops and usually carried a white recognition circle painted on the crown of the forward and aft turrets. In those ships with superfiring aft, and in the case of the *Derfflinger* class, forward superfiring turrets, the circles were painted on the crowns of the superfiring turrets. Also reported was painting over the after funnel during major operations. This was done once outside of the sight of land and repainted grey before returning to port. For the battlecruisers, the aft funnel was not painted over at Dogger Bank but for Jutland major units very possibly could have painted the aft funnel red. A well-known painting of the battleship *König* at Jutland shows her aft funnel painted over in this colour, and there is at least one black and white photo apparently showing *Derfflinger* so painted

**Below:** *Hindenberg* at anchor in Scapa Flow after the Armistice. Although some of the fittings, like searchlights, are hidden by canvas covers, it is a good clear shot of the ship's appearance at the end of the war. *(©National Maritime Museum N29336)*

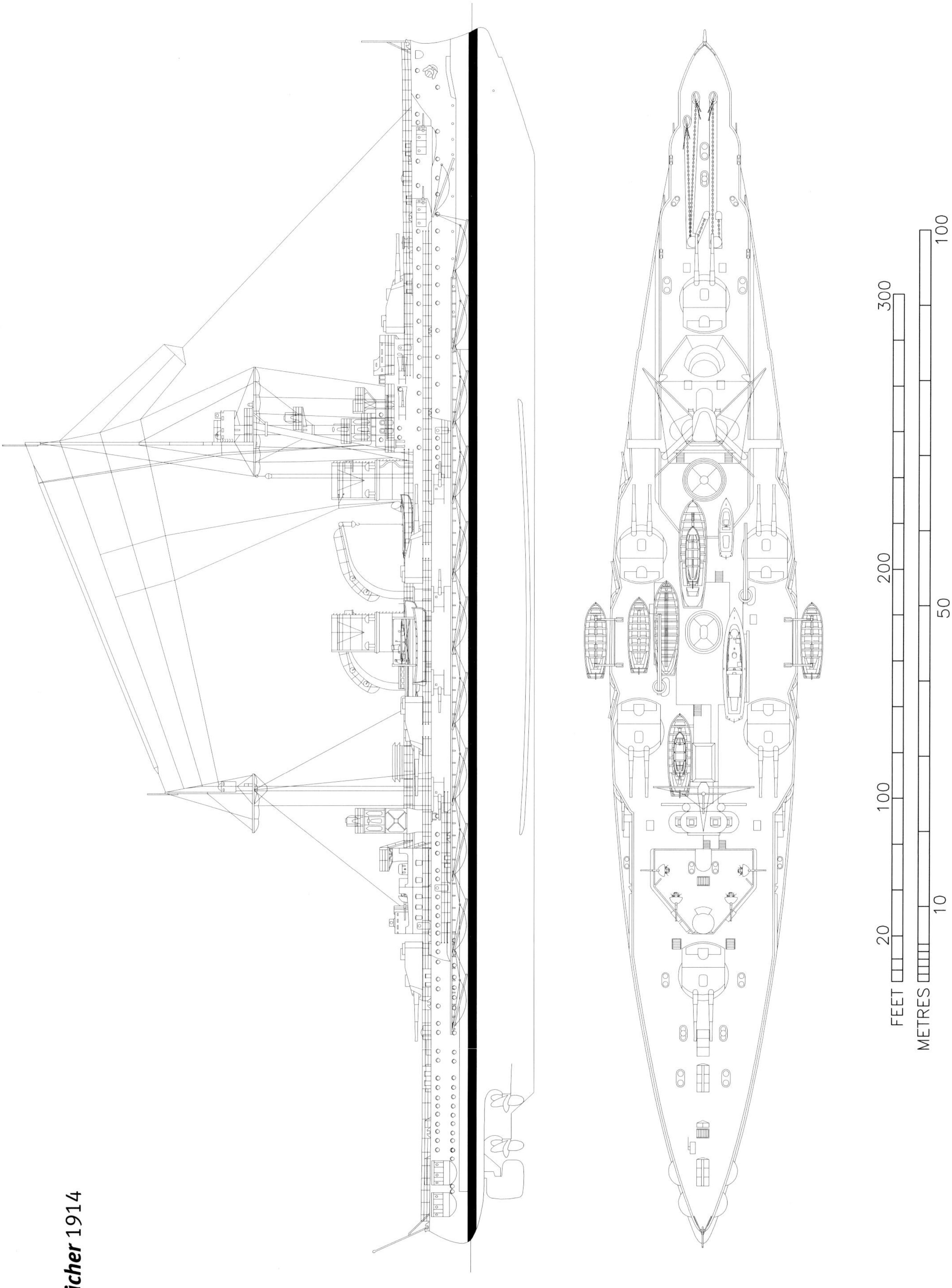


***Blücher*** **1914**

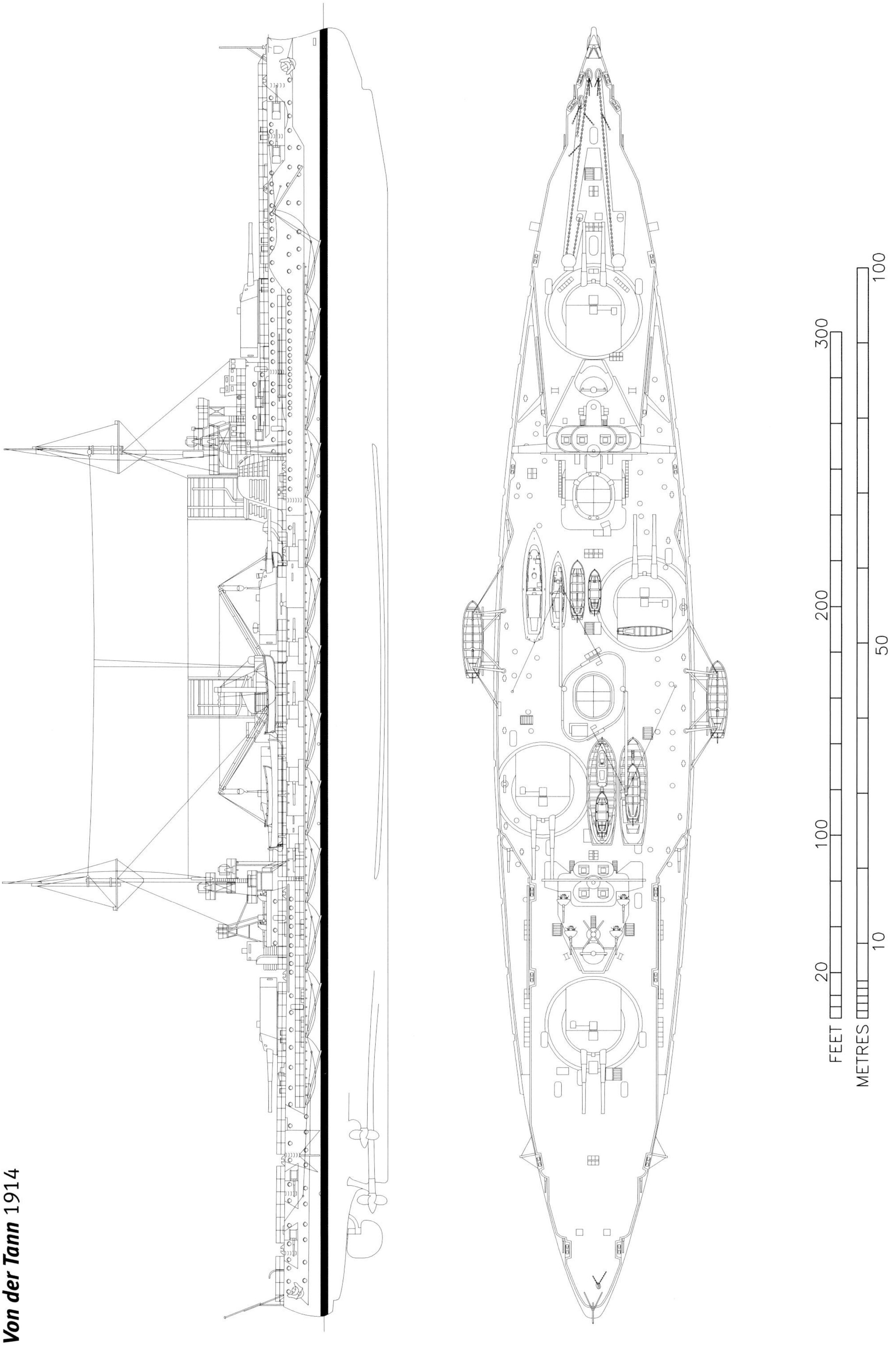


***Von der Tann*** 1914

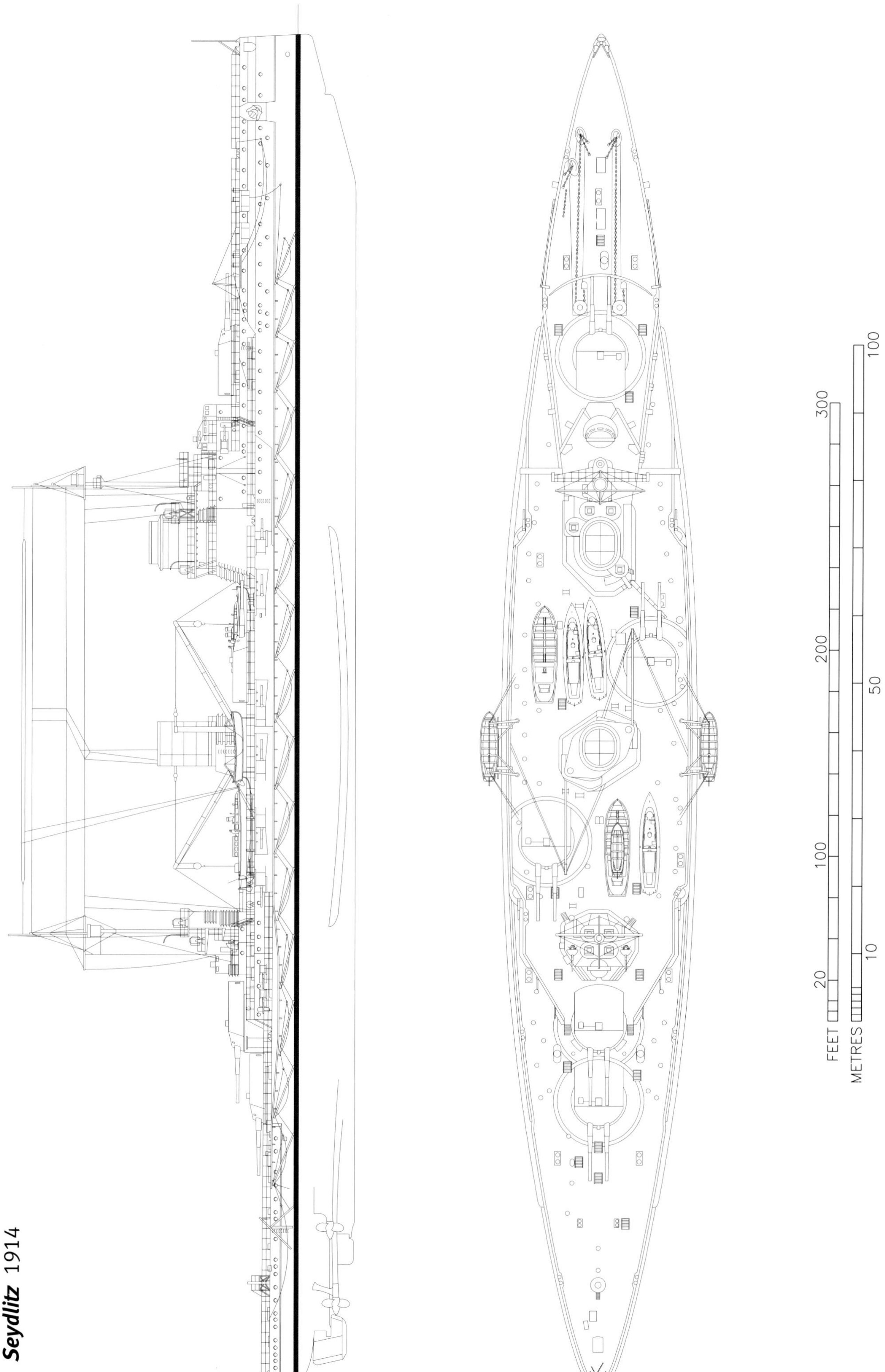


***Seydlitz*** 1914

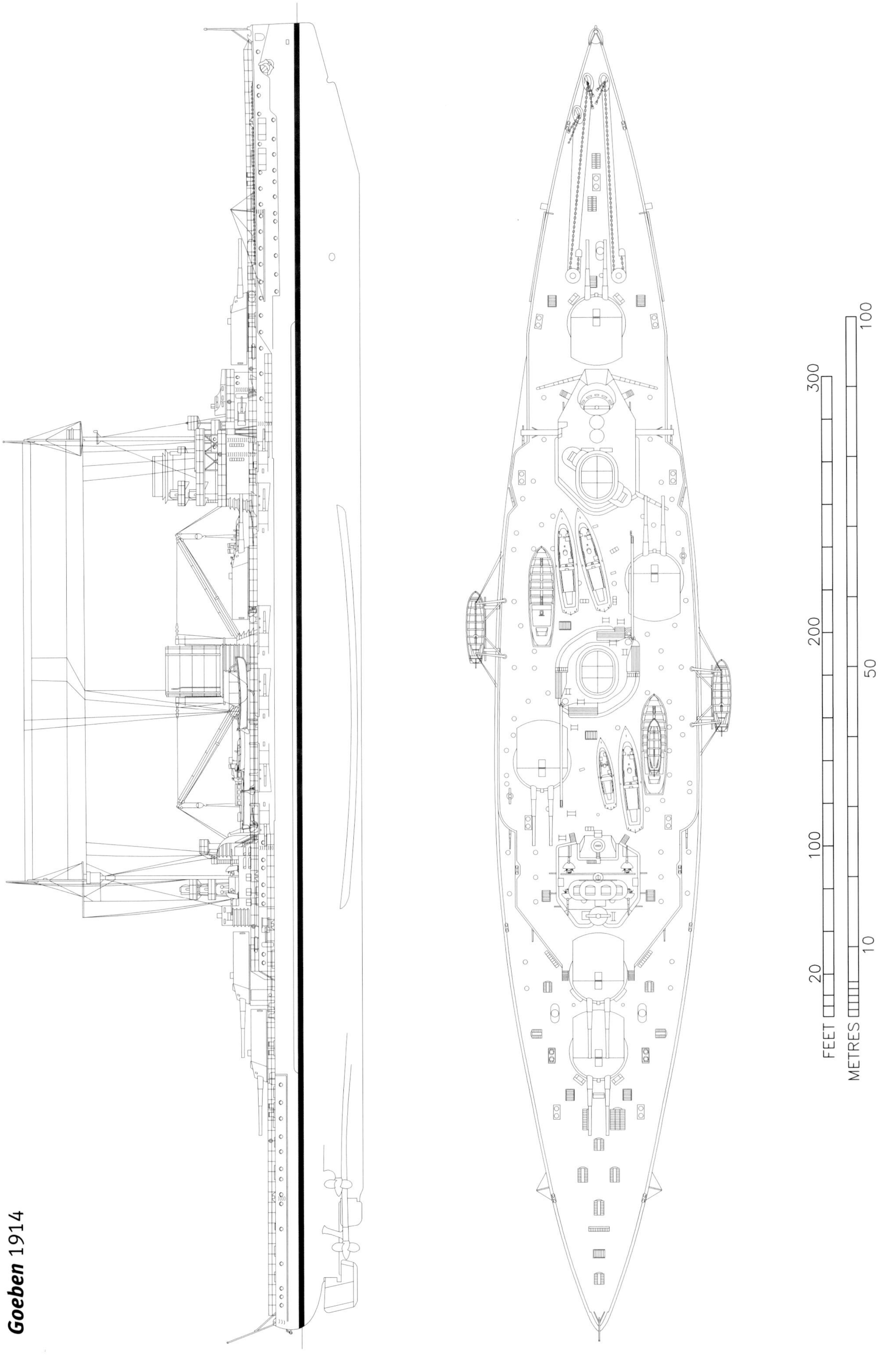


***Goeben* 1914**

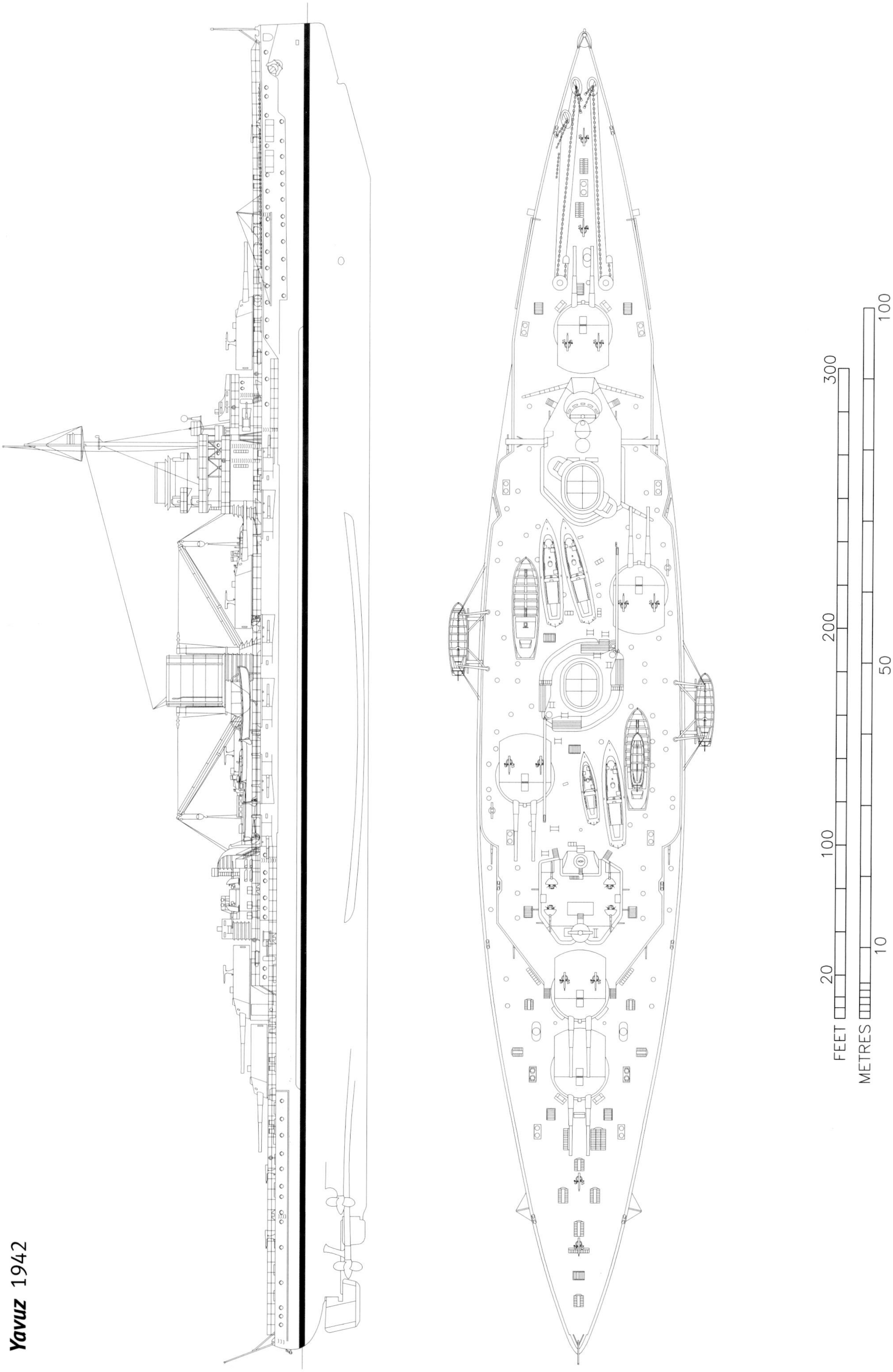


***Yavuz*** 1942

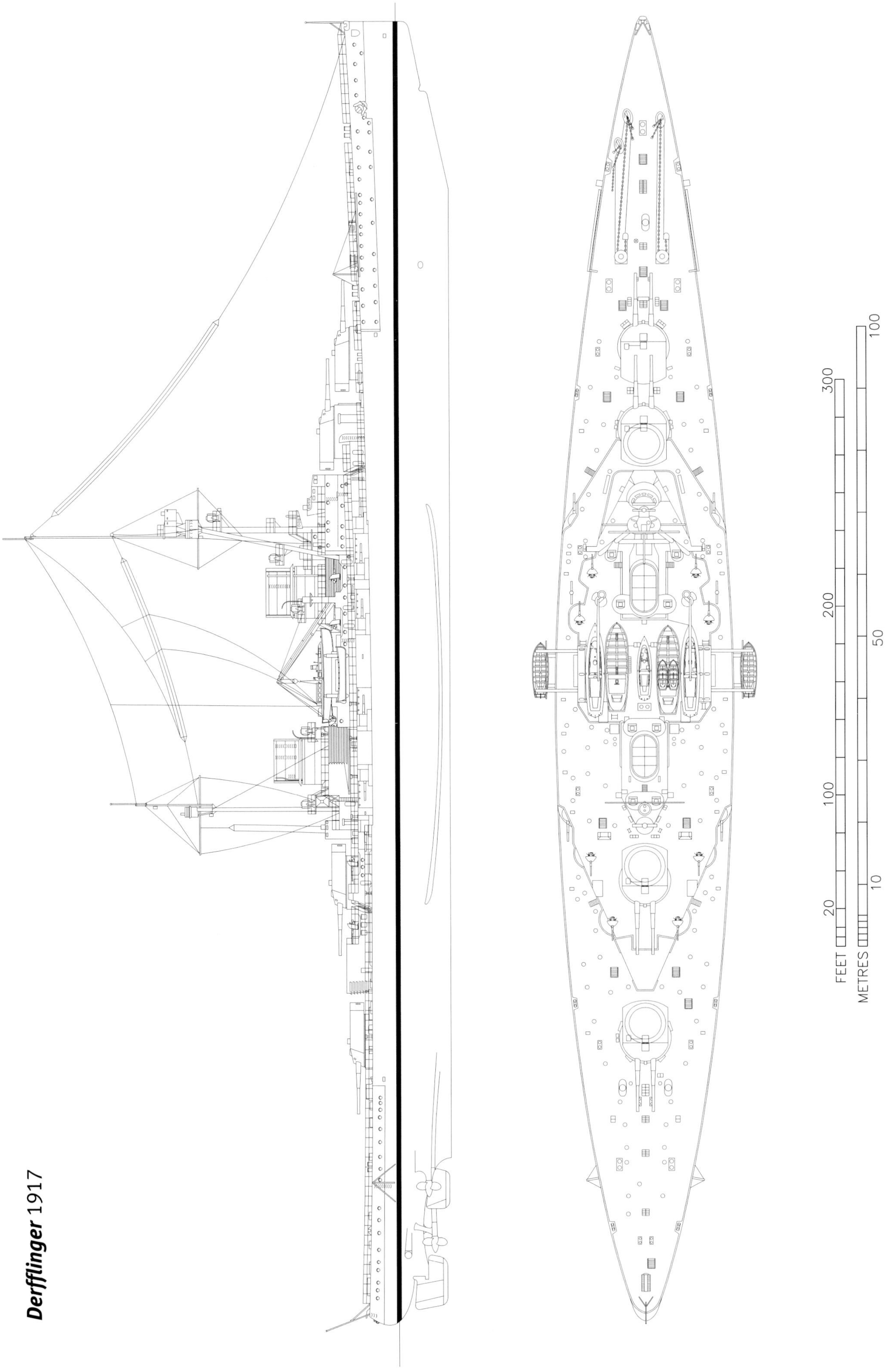


***Derfflinger*** 1917

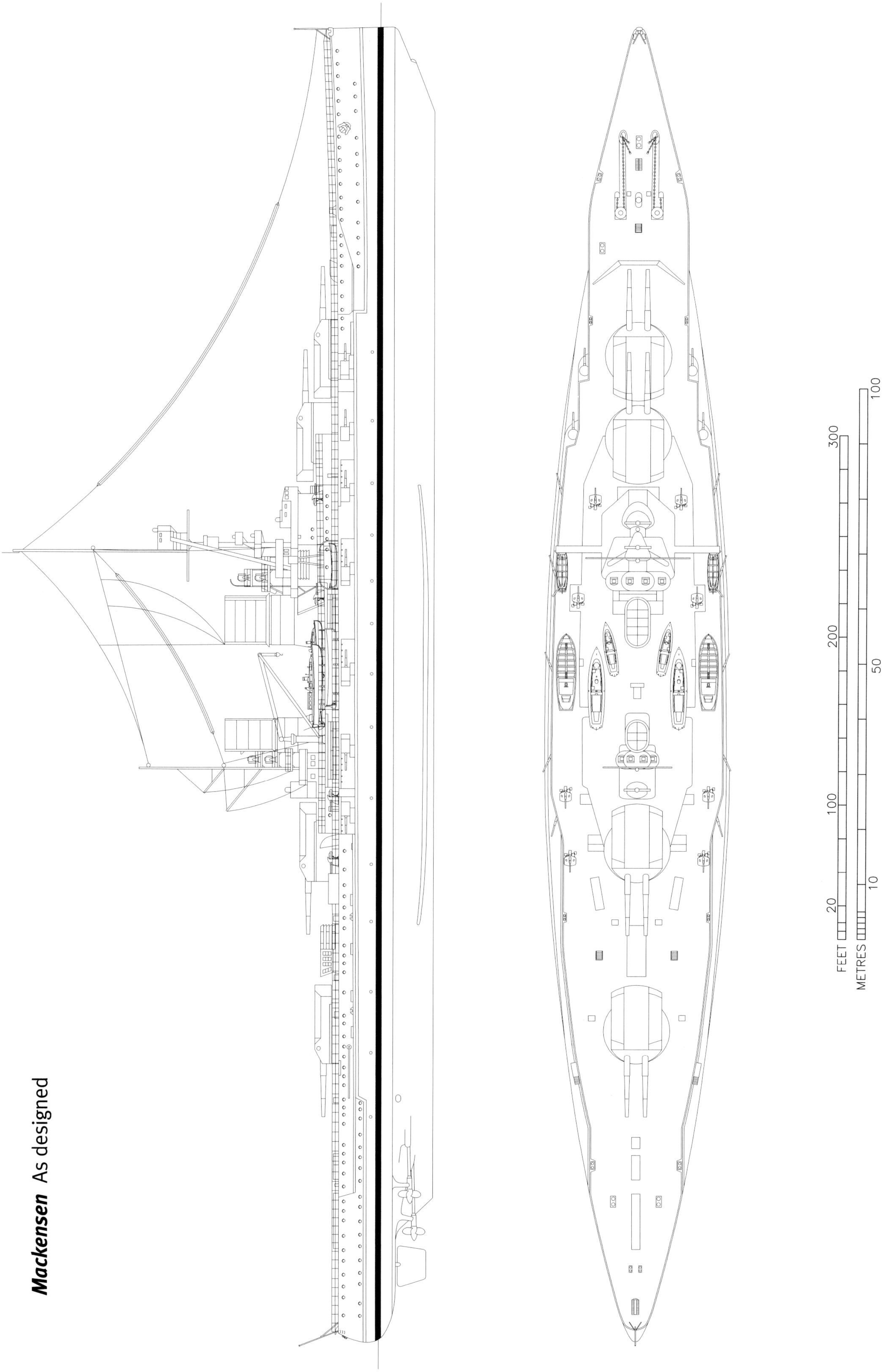


***Mackensen*** As designed

# Selected References

**Barrett, Michael,** *Operation Albion: The German Conquest of the Baltic Islands,* Indiana University Press (Bloomington & Indianapolis, Indiana 2008).
Although only SMS *Moltke* served, as Fleet flagship, in this first successful major amphibious operation, and her active engagement centred around silencing a 12in gun shore battery, the volume of 298 pages makes interesting reading.

**Brice, Martin,** *Warship International,* Fall 1969 (Naval Records Club 1969).
This particular issue of the quarterly journal centred around SMS *Goeben.* The main article includes drawings and bibliography. There is also a short piece on the August 1914 chase of the *Goeben* by Richard Hough, and fourteen pages of photographs from historical sources and taken in 1967 by Aubrey Bowden.

**Breyer, Siegfried,** *Battleships and Battle Cruisers 1905-1970,* Doubleday & Company (Garden City, NY 1973). This massive 480-page anthology of all built or proposed designs of capital ships since HMS *Dreadnought* stresses technical details of the design. There are copious line drawings and tables but no photographs.

**Gröner, Erich**, *German Warships 1815-1945, Volume One: Major Surface Vessels,* first English edition Conway Maritime Press (London 1990); originally published in German as *Die deutschen Kriegsshiffe 1815–1945.* Encyclopedic treatment for all warships of German warships for 140 years. Given the scope of the volume, coverage on each class is limited; many line drawings and tables but no photographs.

**Koop, Gerhard and Schmolke, Klaus-Peter,** *Die Grossen Kreuzer: Von der Tann bis Hindenburg,* Bernard & Graefe Verlag (Bonn 1998).
This German language volume covers all German battlecruiser designs, including the *Mackensen* and *Yorck* classes, 190 pages in length with extensive photographs, maps, line drawings, damage drawings and tables. Even if the reader does not know German, this volume is useful for anyone interested in the subject.

**Legg, Stuart,** *Jutland: An Eyewitness Account of a Great Battle,* The John Day Company, (New York 1966).
This volume of 152 pages uses eyewitness reports of the battle to bring the impressions of the participants in the battle to life. There are no photographs but many maps, six pages of organisational tables and a two-page bibliography are included.

**Marder, Arthur J,** *From the Dreadnought to Scapa Flow,* 5 volumes, reprinted paperback edition Seaforth Publishing (Barnsley 2013–2014).
Surprisingly readable for such an established academic classic, this work is unsurpassed for the breadth of its coverage of naval aspects of the First World War and the previous decade, on the political, administrative and operational levels.

**Massie, Robert,** *Castles of Steel,* Random House (New York 2003).
This volume concerns the entire First World War at sea, including all significant German battlecruiser operations. The volume is 865 pages in length, extensively annotated and unillustrated, and yet it is the most entertaining and informative one-volume general naval history of the war.

**Preston, Anthony,** *Battleships of World War I,* Stackpole Books (Harrisburg, Pennsylvania 1972).
This is a very nice anthology of all capital ship designs used or designed during the First World War, including battle-cruisers and predreadnought battleships. Each class has two to three pages devoted to it with a concise history of the design and careers of each member of the class. The volume is 258 pages in length with line drawings and photographs.

**Ruge, F,** *SMS Seydlitz, Grosser Kreuzer 1913-1919,* Warships in Profile, Volume Two, Doubleday & Company (New York 1973).
This is a bound volume of twelve Warship Profile monographs, SMS *Seydlitz* originally featuring as Warship Profile 14. In 24 pages the author touches on the history of the battlecruiser and then delves into the design and history of the *Seydlitz.* It is handsomely illustrated with numerous photographs and drawings. It also features a two-page colour plate of the ship, as she appeared at the Battle of Jutland.

**Staff, Gary,** *Battle on the Seven Seas: German Cruiser Battles 1914-1918,* Pen & Sword (Barnsley 2011).
This volume covers all battles involving Imperial German cruisers, so the battlecruisers share coverage with light cruisers and von Spee's squadron. The volume is 224 pages in length and supplemented with photographs.

**Staff, Gary,** *German Battlecruisers of World War One: Their Design, Construction and Operations,* Seaforth Publishing (Barnsley 2014).
The most comprehensive coverage of the subject in English, with much original material translated from German official sources. Extensive and detailed text is backed by over 400 illustrations, including full-colour CGI artwork.

**Tarrant, V E,** *Jutland: The German Perspective,* Brockhampton Press (London 1995).
English-language histories of the Battle of Jutland tend to be seen from the perspective of the Royal Navy, but in this volume the author looked at the battle from the German viewpoint. It consists of 318 pages, and is heavily annotated, with numerous warship line drawings, maps and tables.

**Vat, Dan van der,** *The Ship That Changed the World: The Escape of the Goeben to the Dardanelles in 1914,* Hodder and Stoughton (London 1985).
Although subsequent history is included, this volume concentrates on the successful attempt of SMS *Goeben* to evade overwhelming odds in the Mediterranean Sea in August 1914.

## WEBSITES OF MANUFACTURERS

www.artwox.com
shop.modellmarine.de/
www.combrig-models.com/
www.flyhawkmodel.com/html/Flyhawkmodel/
www.goldmm.com/
h-m-v.de/
www.hp-models.com/
ihphobby.tripod.com/
www.ironshipwrights.com
www.lionroar.net/
www.navis-neptun.de/home/home_e.html
www.nntmodell.com/
www.ssnmodellbau.de/
www.tomsmodelworks.com/
shop.vth.de/
www.wsw-modellbau.de/

**Other Websites of Interest**

www.modelwarship.com
www.navymodeling.com
www.steelnavy.com
www.steelnavy.net